Get the Answers to Your Most Important Questions

Why pay someone else for a Tarot reading when you can learn to read the cards yourself?

With the guidance found in this book, you'll learn how to read Tarot cards to answer your most important life questions. Choose from over three dozen spreads developed by a professional Tarot reader:

- Lover's Spread
- Relocation Spread
- Reincarnation Spread
- and many more, including spreads for pregnancy, divorce, legal matters, and career

To be a successful Tarot reader, you need to know what each separate card means—but you also need to be able to look at the larger picture and work them into a meaningful story.

How to Use Tarot Spreads includes dozens of sample readings from the author's personal Tarot practice, showing you how to go beyond card confusion to Tarot inspiration.

About the Author

Sylvia Abraham is owner of The Cosmic Lantern Bookstore in Long Beach, California, where she has been in business selling metaphysical books and supplies for more than 15 years. She has devoted over 20 years to reading the Tarot and teaching others how to interpret the Tarot.

To Write to the Author

If you wish to contact the author or would like more information about this book, please write to the author in care of Llewellyn Worldwide, and we will forward your request. Both the author and publisher appreciate hearing from you and learning of your enjoyment of this book and how it has helped you. Llewellyn Worldwide cannot guarantee that every letter written to the author can be answered, but all will be forwarded. Please write to:

Sylvia Abraham
c/o Llewellyn Worldwide
P.O. Box 64383, Dept. K002-7
St. Paul, MN 55164-0383, U.S.A.

USE TAROT SPREADS

SYLVIA ABRAHAM

Llewellyn Publications
St. Paul, Minnesota

FIRST EDITION
Seventh printing, 2005

Cover Design by Gavin Dayton Duffy
   Cards on cover from Universal Tarot © Lo Scarabeo.
   Used with permission.
Book editing, design, and layout by Astrid Sandell

Library of Congress Cataloging-in-Publication Data
Abraham, Sylvia, 1924-
    How to use tarot spreads : answers to every
questions / Sylvia Abraham. — 1st ed.
        p.   cm.
    ISBN 1-56718-002-7
    1. Tarot. 2. Fortune-telling by cards. I. Title.
BF1879.T2A38   1997
133.3'2424--dc21   97-24733
                                                  CIP

Llewellyn Worldwide does not participate in, endorse, or have any authority or responsibility concerning private business transactions between our authors and the public.
All mail addressed to the author is forwarded but the publisher cannot, unless specifically instructed by the author, give out an address or phone number.

Llewellyn Publications
A Division of Llewellyn Worldwide, Ltd.
P.O. Box 64383, St. Paul, MN 55164-0383
www.llewellyn.com

Printed in the United States of America

Also by Sylvia Abraham

How to Read the Tarot: The Key Word System

CONTENTS

Chapter 1
INTRODUCTION TO TAROT
1

Major and Minor Arcana   4
Court Cards   20
Additional Information   27

Chapter 2
LOVE AND ROMANCE
31

A New Lover   32
A Romantic Attraction   38
Lover's Spread   46
Magical Love   53
Guide for Lovers   62

Chapter 3
HOME AND FAMILY ISSUES
63

Family Problems   64
Health Spread   71
A Thief in the Home   79
Lost Articles Spread   83

Chapter 4
HIGH FINANCES
85

Business Spread   86
Career Spread   94
Lawsuit Spread   104
Money Spread   109
Work Spread   119
Legal Matters Spread   129

Chapter 5
LIFE'S BIG DECISIONS
131

Relationship Problems   132
Marriage Spread   139
Pregnancy Spread   146
Divorce Potential   155

Chapter 6
ON THE MOVE
157

Desire to Move   158
Taking a Trip   166
Relocation Spread   173
Planning a Vacation   176

Chapter 7
SEEKING SELF-KNOWLEDGE
177

All About Me	178
What Is My Destiny?	191
Facing My Fears	198
Old Habit Patterns	204
Information Spread for the Past–Present–Future	208

Chapter 8
SPIRITUAL SEEKERS
211

Spiritual Aspiration	212
Reincarnation Spread	218
Contacting Spirit Guides	230
Soul Mate Spread	238

Chapter 9
JUST FOR FUN
247

Wish Spread	248
Yes or No	258
Magical Lottery Spread	265
Through the Week	270
Tarot Spread Worksheets	271

ACKNOWLEDGMENT

After writing my first book, *How to Read the Tarot: The Key Word System,* a friend suggested I write a book on Tarot spreads. Busy with other projects at the time, I put that idea on the back burner. Suddenly, during the early months of 1995, I found myself involved with writing this book on Tarot spreads! When the time is right, everything falls into place, or so it seems to me.

I want to thank Lynnette for her persistence and her help, and Cathy who gave me a different slant on several of the spreads. My thanks to Gilbert and Phillip for their input and all my other students who participated in this endeavor. I also wish to thank my daughter Lee for her artistic help with the spreads. Several of the spreads concerned family members whom I coaxed into sitting for a reading

For all Tarot readers who may need new ideas about spreads, I hope this book will be helpful. For the new Tarot reader who would like to understand how to read the Tarot, I hope this book fills their needs as well.

Sylvia Abraham

Chapter 1

INTRODUCTION TO TAROT

THERE HAS BEEN MUCH INFORMATION AND conjecture on the beginnings of Tarot, but no conclusive proof of its origins. Many people believe that Tarot was discovered in the fourteenth century and have woven stories around this idea in order to support their premise. One thing is for sure—the Tarot works! The cards have been in use for centuries and that is proof enough of their authenticity.

As a beginner, the more books you read about Tarot, the more confident you will become. The Tarot cards are ideal tools for meditation, and by working with the cards this way you will discover further information about them that you will not find in books.

The following pages provide thumbnail sketches of the upright and reversed meanings of each card based on a system I developed in my book *How to Read the Tarot: The Key Word System*. Some readers prefer to use the cards in their upright meanings only. If it works for them, great! If you wish to use reversed cards in your reading, cut your deck into two parts, turn one in the opposite direction and shuffle the cards together. Have faith, the cards work no matter if upright or reversed. Enjoy the spreads and be sure to try the Magical Lottery spread. Who knows, you could win!

PREPARING A READING

Reading Tarot spreads is easy. Follow the steps outlined below for a positive Tarot reading:

- Select a type of spread that best fits the circumstances the querent (the person you are reading for) would like to examine in the reading.

- Have the querent shuffle the deck of Tarot cards. Ask the person to make a wish and concentrate on their question. If they desire, they can cut the cards.

- Have the querent hand the cards back to you, the reader.

- Lay the cards out according to the format of the selected spread.

- Look over the spread and check for repeated elements:

  How many Wands appear?
  How many Cups?
  How many Pentacles?
  How many Swords?

- Check the numbers of each card and notice if those are repeated.

- Are there many Major Arcana or Court Cards? If there are, then too many people are involved in the querent's life.

- Read the cards either right side up or reversed, depending on how they fall in the spread. Some readers will read the cards using only the upright meanings. If it works, fine!

- Try to end the reading on a positive note, but be as truthful as possible.

- Do not read too many spreads for the same person on a single day—it will create confusion in that person's mind. Tell this individual that they must wait a week before you read for them again.

Note: If any cards falls out of the deck during shuffling, be sure to read those as well. All of these cards have information concerning the querent. Check the bottom card of the deck after you have laid out the spread; there is a message there as well.

Beginner Tarot readers: Read through the book first and then try your skill at reading the spreads. Experience is the best teacher and reading for others hones your talents and enhances your intuition. Trust yourself always.

The reader has an obligation to the client which must not be taken lightly. Be responsible with the information and be blessed.

THE TAROT

Major and Minor Arcana

THE FOOL 0

Key Word: EVERYONE

Upright: I desire new experiences and adventures. A need for caution. Watch your footing.

Reversed: Lacking confidence. Take responsibility for actions. Curb anxiety, release fears.

THE MAGICIAN I

Key Words: I WILL

Upright: I will have new beginnings in many directions. Leadership potential. New growth.

Reversed: I will not have new beginnings at this time. Lack of ambition or drive. Strong sexual focus.

The four Aces have the same key words as THE MAGICIAN: I WILL.

ACE OF WANDS

Upright: I will have new beginnings in my work and social life. New opportunities. A birth.

Reversed: I will not have new beginnings in my work or social life. Trips deferred. Plans canceled.

ACE OF CUPS

Upright: I will have new beginnings in love relationships. New residence. Happiness. Emotionally upbeat. Peace and good health.

Reversed: I will not have new beginnings in love. Emotional instability. Loss. Separation.

ACE OF PENTACLES
Upright: I will have new beginnings with money. Prosperity. Inheritance. Raise in pay.
Reversed: I will not have new beginnings with money. Financial picture gloomy. Greed. Jealousy.

ACE OF SWORDS
Upright: I will have new beginnings in problems and troubles. Loss. Potential for operation.
Reversed: I will not have new beginnings in problems and troubles. Remove old ideas. Be confident.

HIGH PRIESTESS II
Key Words: I KNOW
Upright: I know about the world and its duality. Memory, reason, secrets, and the subconscious.
Reversed: I don't know about the world. Close minded. Unskilled. Selfish, fearful, and egotistical.

The four twos have the same key words as the HIGH PRIESTESS: I KNOW.

TWO OF WANDS
Upright: I know my work and social activities. Having the world in my hand. Success in business. Confidence.
Reversed: I don't know my work or place in society. Unbalanced actions, fear of failure. Lacking skills.

TWO OF CUPS

Upright: I know about love and emotions. A good relationship is emotionally healthy. Birth. Happy events.

Reversed: I know nothing about love. Unhappy emotions. Sexual problems. Loss or separation. Health issues.

TWO OF PENTACLES

Upright: I know how to balance my money. Financial gain. Budgets work. Prosperity minded. Good health.

Reversed: I don't know how to handle money. Spendthrift. Depression over finances. Poverty minded.

TWO OF SWORDS

Upright: I know my problems and troubles and don't wish to see them. Fear of being hurt. Unclear thinking.

Reversed: I don't know my problems and troubles and don't want to see them. Illusory thinking. Fear of new knowledge.

THE EMPRESS III

Key Words: I MAKE

Upright: I make my experiences. I create my happiness, my enjoyment, and my life. Pregnancy is a potential. Could represent my mother or an older female.

Reversed: I don't make myself happy. I don't use my creative talents. Problems with mother or other females. No pregnancy. Lacking confidence.

The four threes have the same key words as THE EMPRESS: I MAKE.

THREE OF WANDS
Upright: I make my work and social life. Creatively visualizing new work and good times socially.
Reversed: I don't make my work or social activities. Lacking faith in personal abilities. Unhappiness.

THREE OF CUPS
Upright: I make myself happy doing what I like. Good with friends. Pregnancy. Marriage.
Reversed: I don't make myself happy in love. An emotional drain. Miscarriage. Liquor or drug problems. Loneliness.

THREE OF PENTACLES
Upright: I make my money. I am a master craftsman. Creative talents bring financial rewards.
Reversed: I don't make money. Over-qualified or underpaid at my job. Health and money are problems.

THREE OF SWORDS
Upright: I make my problems and troubles. A love triangle. Shedding tears. Separation or divorce.
Reversed: I don't make my problems or troubles. Rival. Feeling stabbed in the back. Deceit.

THE EMPEROR IV
Key Words: I REALIZE

Upright: I realize I am the boss, leader, and initiator. I am original. I am a father figure. Action, balance, stability, and power.
Reversed: I don't realize who I am. Lacking authority. Immature. Inexperienced and unstable.

The four fours have the same key words as The
EMPEROR: I REALIZE.

FOUR OF WANDS
Upright: I realize my work and social activities. Balanced work and home situations. Marriage.
Reversed: I do not realize imbalances in my home or
work environment. Lack of prosperity. Not a fruitful time.

FOUR OF CUPS
Upright: I realize my past love and emotional experiences. Old habit patterns are holding me back from
being involved with new relationships.
Reversed: I do not realize my emotions are being
drained. Disappointed in love. Feeling rejected.
Some loss. Broken relationship.

FOUR OF PENTACLES
Upright: I realize the value of money. Avarice. Selling
property. Faith in material possessions.
Reversed: I do not realize the value of money.
Spendthrift. Gambling. A need to balance the budget.

FOUR OF SWORDS
Upright: I realize my problems and troubles. Rest
from strife. Need faith to overcome struggles.
Reversed: I don't realize my problems and troubles.
Burning the candle at both ends. Health issues.

THE HIEROPHANT V
Key Words: I BELIEVE
Upright: I believe in my Higher Self. Resenting

authority or control by others. Need to meditate. Inner guidance.

Reversed: I do not believe in an inner teacher. Indulgent, pleasure seeker, and materialistic.

The four fives have the same key words as THE HIEROPHANT: I BELIEVE.

FIVE OF WANDS

Upright: I believe in work and social activities. I believe in my ideas, will, and ego over others.

Reversed: I don't believe in the work or society. Disharmony. Little faith in own abilities or ego.

FIVE OF CUPS

Upright: I believe in love but have a fear of commitment. Crying over spilled milk. Broken romance.

Reversed: I don't believe in love or romance. An emotional crisis. Divorce or separation. Death.

FIVE OF PENTACLES

Upright: I believe in money, it is my god. Unemployment. Crippling ideas. Drugs. Poverty minded.

Reversed: I don't believe that money is my god. A new job or work that is more difficult. Seek your inner guide.

FIVE OF SWORDS

Upright: I believe in problems and troubles. Empty victory. Loss of friends through cruelty.

Reversed: I don't believe in problems or troubles for myself or others. Seeking mental balance.

THE LOVERS VI

Key Words: I CHOOSE

Upright: I choose my life. Seeking answers from a Higher Self. Knowing the positive and the negative in life. A trip or social event.

Reversed: Other people make my choices. Engagement or marriage plans delayed. Little trust in self.

The four sixes have the same key words as THE LOVERS: I CHOOSE.

SIX OF WANDS

Upright: I choose my work and social activities. Victory! Right use of ego and will.

Reversed: I don't make choices at work or socially. Temptations overcome common sense. Delays.

SIX OF CUPS:

Upright: I make choices in my love relationships. I choose to control my emotions. Potential to live in the past, or someone from the past returns. New love affair or marriage.

Reversed: Others make decisions for me. An emotionally draining situation. Loss. Divorce. Health problems.

SIX OF PENTACLES

Upright: I make choices with my money. Desire to be fair and share resources. Helping others.

Reversed: I don't make choices with my money. Poverty minded. Not charitable. Health matters.

SIX OF SWORDS

Upright: I choose my problems and troubles. I am tempted to run away rather than face my problems.
Reversed: I have no choice to make about my problems and troubles. I must stay and face the situation. No trips at this time.

THE CHARIOT VII

Key Words: THE PATH
Upright: The mental path will take me to victory. I control my senses through my mind. The Charioteer is my Higher Self and I trust It.
Reversed: Unwise path. Focus is on the material aspect, not mental. Self-indulgence. Opinionated.

The four sevens have the same key words as THE CHARIOTEER: THE PATH.

SEVEN OF WANDS

Upright: Taking the mental path in my work and social life. Success and victory in business. Feeling superior at work. New ideas. Loner.
Reversed: No victory at work or socially. Feeling inferior or incompetent. Material desires. Drugs.

SEVEN OF CUPS

Upright: Victory gained in love. Creative visualization versus daydreams. Mental control over emotions. Liquor or drugs not positive.
Reversed: Defeat through love and emotional needs. Loss or separation. Little trust or faith in self.

SEVEN OF PENTACLES
Upright: Path of money leads to victory. Financial responsibilities. Prosperity minded. Confidence.
Reversed: Uncertain path to money. Poverty minded. Little money sense. Health affected by negativity.

SEVEN OF SWORDS
Upright: Path leads to problems and troubles. Temporary situation. Feeling cheated or some loss.
Reversed: Path of problems and troubles not mentally clear. Jealousy. Unhappy relationship. Situation not over at this time.

STRENGTH VIII
Key Word: STRENGTH
Upright: Having the strength to overcome any difficulties. Courage and endurance. Creative. Control over desires.
Reversed: Lacking strength. Little self-control. Egotistical and vain. Not trustworthy. Shallow.

The four eights have the same keyword as STRENGTH: STRENGTH

EIGHT OF WANDS
Upright: I have the strength to do my work and be involved in my social life. Messages regarding work. Travel for work or pleasure.
Reversed: Lacking strength in work or social activities. Delays and frustrations. No travel plans.

EIGHT OF CUPS
Upright: I have strength in my love and emotions. A search for spiritual values. Turning my back on temptations. Letting go of past experiences.
Reversed: Lacking strength in love and emotions. Emotional drain due to loss, separation, or divorce.

EIGHT OF PENTACLES
Upright: Having the strength to make money. The apprentice. Learning new skills. More confident.
Reversed: Not having the strength to wait for money. Desire for quick money. Criminal activities. Dislike of hard work.

EIGHT OF SWORDS
Upright: Having the strength to cope with problems and troubles. In bondage. On unsafe ground. Potential for health problems.
Reversed: Lack of strength in handling troubles or problems. Feeling unsafe in the midst of chaos. Let go of unhealthy situations now.

THE HERMIT IX
Upright: Using the wisdom of my experiences in positive ways. Inner teacher. New lessons in my life. Meetings with an older person.
Reversed: Lack of wisdom through my experiences. Selfish and intolerant. Sexual inhibitions. Fear.

The four nines have the same key words as THE HERMIT: WISDOM THROUGH EXPERIENCE.

NINE OF WANDS
Upright: Using wisdom in work and socially. Ability to protect self through wisdom in business or relationships. Using fair tactics at work.
Reversed: Lack of wisdom or experiences in the work or socially. Open to abuse from outside sources.

NINE OF CUPS
Upright: The wish card! If up—you get your wish. Wisdom through experience in love and emotions.
Reversed: You don't get your wish at this time. Emotional drain. Lacking wisdom. Loss or separation.

NINE OF PENTACLES
Upright: Wisdom through experience with money. Independence. Inheritance. Healthy existence.
Reversed: Lack of wisdom through experience with money. Dependency brings depression. Spendthrift.

NINE OF SWORDS
Upright: Experiences in problems and troubles bring wisdom. Despair. A crisis period. Loss. Illness.
Reversed: Experiences have not brought wisdom or understanding. Problems and troubles can worsen. Little confidence. Have faith.

WHEEL OF FORTUNE X
Key Words: CHANGES AND NEW CYCLES
Upright: Time to make changes, take a gamble or make plans to travel. Marriage potential.
Reversed: Changes not happening now. Cycle not finished. Take care of health and diet.

The four tens have the same key words as THE WHEEL OF FORTUNE: CHANGES AND NEW CYCLES.

TEN OF WANDS
Upright: Major changes at work or socially. Laying down burdens. New business methods. Travel.
Reversed: No changes at this time. Don't gamble. Obstacles are frustrating. Back problems.

TEN OF CUPS
Upright: Changes in love and emotions. New cycle in family relations. A move or short trip.
Reversed: An emotional drain through family affairs. Overindulgence results in ill health. Loss, separation, or divorce. Unhappiness.

TEN OF PENTACLES
Upright: Major changes in finances. New home, job, or inheritance. Success in money matters.
Reversed: No changes in finances. Misfortune with money. Older people may be a burden.

TEN OF SWORDS
Upright: Big changes in problems and troubles. Burdens may be removed. Back problems are relieved. Cycle of negativity may be ending.
Reversed: No changes in problems and troubles. Need to have courage to face difficulties. Situation not as negative as it seems.

JUSTICE XI

Key Words: *JUSTICE, EQUILIBRIUM*

Upright: Balance, law, harmony, karma, and fairness. Seeking justice in business or personally. A successful legal battle. Potential marriage.

Reversed: Legal complications due to anger and hostilities. Prejudiced views. Overconfidence can lead to failure. Depression. Health affected.

HANGED MAN XII

Key Words: *SACRIFICE, REVERSAL*

Upright: Sacrificed to the will and desires of others. In bondage to personal views. Trials and duties to family. Keep feet on the ground. Meditate.

Reversed: Procrastination. Fooled by others. Little or no trust in a higher power. Drugs or liquor used to escape. Illusionary.

DEATH XIII

Key Words: *TRANSFORMATION*

Upright: End of a situation. Change for the better. New ideas and future plans are healthy. Money comes to you. Be open to love. Enlightenment.

Reversed: Stagnation, frustration, and unhappiness. No transformation. Lost love. Jealousy, anger, and resentment can affect health.

TEMPERANCE XIV

Key Words: *MODERATION, TESTS, TRIALS*

Upright: Positive use of energy, self-control, and har-

mony. Trusting the inner self for guidance. Patience during difficult experiences. Meditate.
Reversed: Self-indulgent, restless, and little control over emotions. Negative use of sexual energy. Ignorance of higher laws and little faith.

THE DEVIL XV

Key Words: *MATERIALISM AND DECEPTION*

Upright: Bound to the world by physical and material greed. Desire for social success. Acceptance at any cost. Creative energy wasted in pleasure.
Reversed: Less selfishness or greed. Desire to lift the veil of illusion. Accepting responsibility for actions. Change diet for better health.

THE TOWER XVI

Key Word: *CATASTROPHE*

Upright: Overthrow of false ideas. Out with old habit patterns. Strife and discord in relationships. Stop critical or judgmental speech for a happier life.
Reversed: Refusing to change old habit patterns. Sexual needs, resentment, and jealousy cause catastrophes.

THE STAR XVII

Key Words: *DISCOVERY AND ASPIRATION*

Upright: Faith and trust in life. Setting new goals. New opportunities. Optimistic. Using skills.
Reversed: Pessimistic regarding career moves, relationships and life in general. Not setting new goals for the future. Health matters. Low self-esteem.

THE MOON XVIII

Key Word: ATTAINMENT

Upright: Deception and illusion regarding personal attainment. A slow but steady climb to enlightenment is assured. Overcoming fears from subconscious memories. Psychic ability. Person can feel victimized by others.

Reversed: Depression due to delayed plans. Feeling betrayed. Unconscious actions. Not seeing or hearing truth.

THE SUN XIX

Key Word: RENEWAL

Upright: Seeking truth and happiness. New work in science or mathematics. Open to new thought. Self-confidence. Optimism and courage.

Reversed: Lacks courage or confidence. Sexual needs are major issues. Dishonesty creates discord. Loss of trust from others. Ostentatiousness.

JUDGMENT XX

Key Word: AWARENESS

Upright: Faith in a higher power within. New knowledge brings joy and happiness. Not accepting traditional views. Change of residence, new position or career. Health improvement.

Reversed: Materialistic approach to life. Blind faith and mistaken judgment. Tunnel vision. Loss or separation from family. Health matters arise.

THE WORLD XXI

Key Word: COSMIC CONSCIOUSNESS

Upright: Success in all endeavors. Goals attained. Long journey proves beneficial. A new job, career change, or move. Feeling supported by inner resources. Victory. Balance.

Reversed: No success or material gain. Plans delayed or defeated. Lacking vision or truth. Fear of change or the unknown. Little mental growth.

COURT CARDS

There are sixteen Court cards. These cards refer to people in your life and can indicate a relationship, members of your family, people at work, or relatives. They may also indicate "ideas" that are in your thoughts. If the last card in a spread is a Court card it can mean that someone else must make the final decision for you.

KINGS

Age 35 or older. Kings signify a father figure, authority, wisdom, and experience.

QUEENS

Age 35 or older. Queens signify a mother image. She is an authority figure and indicates maturity, nurturing, and understanding.

Note: If a King or Queen is reversed in a spread, the card may represent a negative person. Also, the King reversed may indicate a female of that card's particular corresponding astrological sign (positive or negative). The Queen reversed may indicate a male of that card's particular sign (positive or negative).

KNIGHTS

Age 25 to 40. Knights are messengers. When the card is upright, it refers to a male or a positive message. The Knight of Swords, upright, is the exception and the message is not usually pleasant. This card reversed will indicate a female of that particular astrological sign.

PAGES
Age 1 to 25. Pages represent children in various stages of growth and inexperience. They can indicate messengers, schoolchildren, young adults, and assorted problems. At times, a Page upright could denote a male and reversed, a female. In a reading it is sometimes difficult to say, "Do you have a son or daughter?" At times the Page indicates a feminine male child or a strong female child. The Pages can be deceptive!

Divinatory Meanings

KING OF WANDS
Upright: This King is independent, influential, and an authority figure. He is ambitious, with executive talents and leadership qualities. He has good ideas. He is an Aries type.
Reversed: This King is childish, dependent, and has anti-social attitudes. He can be selfish and domineering—a petty tyrant.

KING OF CUPS
Upright: This King is emotional, loving, caring, and nurturing. A good family man when married. He needs to feel safe and secure in his professional and personal life. He is a Cancer type.
Reversed: This King is cold, uncaring, and not nurturing. He can be untrustworthy in business or with relationships. Potential to be ruthless and calculating.

KING OF PENTACLES
Upright: The King of Pentacles is a good financial

adviser, practical, and reliable. He is slow to anger but can be very stubborn. Good in business, banking, and sales. He is a Taurus type.

Reversed: This King is selfish, lazy, a speculator, and impractical. He loves luxury, is sensual, and desires pleasure. He can be dishonest and his value judgment may be peculiar.

KING OF SWORDS

Upright: This King is a professional man, a lawyer, or in the military. This card can also indicate the querent's need for a lawyer. He has mental dexterity and is a good counselor with lots of nervous energy. He is a Gemini type.

Reversed: This King is fickle and superficial. He dissipates his energy. He is unkind, a gossip, and unstable. He rebels against authority. Potential loss in a lawsuit.

QUEEN OF WANDS

Upright: This Queen desires success in work and her social life. She is an authority figure—ambitious and ego-driven. This Queen needs admiration and attention. Leo type female.

Reversed: This Queen is domineering, demanding, and controlling at work and in social situations. She is unloving, lacks humor, and has a large ego. She can be resentful, angry, and jealous. This Queen can be ruthless.

QUEEN OF CUPS

Upright: This Queen speaks of love and her emotional needs. She is a good wife and mother, very protective of her family. Sex is important to her well-being. This Queen is intuitive, intense, and powerful. A Scorpio type female.

Reversed: This Queen is dishonest in love. Her emotions are drained due to a loss, separation, or any other negative event. She has a terrible temper, likes intrigue, and can be jealous of others. Potential to be unfaithful.

QUEEN OF PENTACLES

Upright: Making money is the focus for this Queen. She is an idealist and perfectionistic. She also has critical views. This is harvest time after much labor. This Queen works with health issues. Potential for pregnancy. Gifts from family. Sexual focus. Virgo type female.

Reversed: This Queen is a spendthrift and lazy. She is a superficial friend, lacks confidence, and is judgmental. She feels imperfect and limits her prosperity. Physical and material focus.

QUEEN OF SWORDS

Upright: Problems and troubles are the focus for this Queen. She represents a divorced woman or a widow. This Queen is strong-willed, sharp-tongued, and temperamental. She desires a relationship. Legal problems may confront her. She must make decisions. A Libra type female.

Reversed: This Queen has problems and troubles but does not wish to see them. She fears divorce or separation. Her sexual needs drive her to a relationship. The Queen is not always open or honest.

KNIGHT OF WANDS
Upright: This messenger brings information regarding work and social activities. Good news concerning the job, planning a trip, or a change of residence. New interests, glad tidings. Leo type energy. Time to shine.
Reversed: The messenger does not arrive or the news is not positive. Some delays causing frustration and depression. Expectations not fulfilled.

KNIGHT OF CUPS
Upright: Positive messages regarding love and emotional needs. The Knight brings new information about a birth, invitation to a party or wedding. The Knight is a loving, sensual, and sexual person. Scorpio type energy. Travel Plans.
Reversed: Messages concerning love did not arrive. Invitations, notices of marriages, or birth announcements were not received. An emotional drain involving relationships, friendships, or family. Some loss or a separation.

KNIGHT OF PENTACLES
Upright: Messages regarding finances are received. Good news about an inheritance, real estate, or other valuables. This Knight shows good health and vitality. He enjoys material possessions and sensual pleasures. He has many desires. Taurus type energy. Money used for good times.
Reversed: Messages about money not received or positive. Lack of financial well-being. Delays. Poverty minded. Being lazy, indulgent, and over-sexed causes negative experiences in life.

KNIGHT OF SWORDS

Upright: This messenger brings news of problems and troubles. These messages may relate to you personally or others close to you. Rage, anger, and frustration are in the message. Mental aggression may cause physical problems. Aquarius-type energy. Think positively.

Reversed: Messages of problems or troubles may have gone astray. Messages concerning invitations, notices of marriage or birth, or love did not arrive. Travel plans. The Knight is close-minded and unreliable. Lacking discrimination in dealing with others. Wild accusations. The focus may be too physical rather than mental. Some loss or a separation. This Knight refers to the "mental" plane and they can spout and sputter but with very little result. It can mean "all talk and no action."

PAGE OF WANDS

Upright: This Page is eager to experience work and social life. He or she desires freedom, is headstrong, a wanderer. This Page has great expectations and some luck from the gods. Travel, foreign people, and philosophy are some of their needs. Sagittarius type energy.

Reversed: This Page can be lazy, immoral, and refuse to work. He or she can be fickle, faithless, cruel, and extravagant. The Page can be a gossip and a betrayer of confidences.

PAGE OF CUPS

Upright: This Page refers to love and emotions. He or she has psychic abilities and is creative. They can be healers. The Page brings good news concerning love relationships, parties, marriages, and births. Pisces type energy.

Reversed: A lack of love and an emotional drain is seen with this Page. He or she has great expectations which may not be fulfilled. Unhappy news regarding a relationship. Potential for emotional abuse. Not using creative talents.

PAGE OF PENTACLES

Upright: This Page desires money. This is the card of the scholar. He or she wants financial security, to pursue a career, become a professional, and make it to the top. They are ambitious, materialistic, and traditional. Desire for gain. Capricorn type energy. Education will help.

Reversed: This Page is not interested in work or school and will not set goals. They are lazy, selfish, greedy, and desire the easy life. The messages from this Page are not positive and can refer to health matters.

PAGE OF SWORDS

Upright: This Page refers to problems and troubles. He or she desires new and novel experiences. New knowledge and many friendships. This Page is extroverted, naive, and unconventional. This person is motivated by concern for others. Aquarius type energy. Be aware of self.

Reversed: Problems and troubles descend on this Page due to his or her lack of attention. Friendships and relationships may not be too important to this Page. They are apt to be anxious, introverted, and paranoid.

ADDITIONAL INFORMATION

Following is some additional information concerning correspondences of the Tarot cards which can be helpful in the readings.

The information in the following table can be applied to the last card of the spread, allowing you to tell the querent when an event may take place. A reader should have some idea how long the information is in effect. Information gained in a typical reading can last a month, a year, or a lifetime. The information becomes a part of the querent's thinking and they rarely forget what a reader has told them—positive or negative.

SYMBOL	TIME	SEASONS	ELEMENT
Wands	weeks	Spring	fire
Cups	days	Summer	water
Pentacles	years	Winter	earth
Swords	months	Fall	air

ASTROLOGICAL SIGNS

There are many good books on astrology and learning more about the signs can deepen your knowledge regarding the cards. It can also indicate a certain person coming into or leaving the querent's life. What follows is a simple description of the traits of each sign and their correspondences within the Tarot suits.

Zodiac correspondences:

Wands:	Aries, Leo, Sagittarius
Cups:	Cancer, Scorpio, Pisces
Pentacles:	Taurus, Virgo, Capricorn
Swords:	Gemini, Libra, Aquarius

Aries: This is a fire sign which means "action and energy." These people are always on the go. They insist on making changes. They can be childlike, independent, courageous, and may have leadership qualities.

Taurus: This is an earth sign which refers to materialism, physicality, and inertia. These people can work, earn their daily bread, and enjoy the fruits of their labor. They can also be lazy, stolid, stubborn, and over-indulgent.

Gemini: This is an air sign which is mental. These people are thinkers, daydreamers, superficial, and charming. They are tricksters, not always grounded, and love to chatter about any subject.

Cancer: This is a water sign referring to emotions, intuition, nurturing, sensitivity, and caring. These people are called the mothers of the earth. They enjoy home life, real estate, and security.

Leo: This is a fire sign indicating energy and action. These people want the spotlight, applause, and attention. They have great expectations and are usually disappointed. This is the sign of the ego and is considered the strongest sign of the zodiac.

Virgo: This is an earth sign—physical, material, and stubborn. These people are the workers of the zodiac. They deal with health issues, also. They are critical, judgmental, and perfectionistic. They are always looking for flaws at work, and are often disappointed in people.

Libra: This is an air sign, mental. These people seek equality, justice, friends, and lovers. They tend to be in love with love. They rarely find what they are seeking because they are not balanced in their own lives. They do not treat others with equality or justice. They are creative.

Scorpio: This is a water sign—intense, possessive, jealous, sexual, and vengeful. They feel intensely, are sensitive and emotional. They enjoy working with other people's money or possessions. These people can be very powerful, carry the "sting of death" within them, and must be transformed during their lifetime.

Sagittarius: This is a fire sign—action and energy. This is a freedom sign, one who can travel the world with a pack on their back, mixing with a variety of people, learning new philosophies, and getting a higher education. They make their moral code in the moment and rarely stay in relationships for long.

Capricorn: This is an earth sign—physical and material. All Capricorns are noted for their desire to succeed. They want a successful social life and lots of money and material possessions. These are priorities in their lives. Unfortunately, Capricorns will do most anything to get ahead, legal or otherwise. They are persistent, which adds to their success.

Aquarius: This is an air sign—mental. This is the sign of brotherhood, friends, hopes, and wishes. These people are inventive, usually positive, and desire to be of service and help humanity. The Aquarian age is upon us and we hope it will bring peace and brotherly love into every heart.

Pisces: This is a water sign, emotional, sensitive, creative, and very psychic. These people have many outlets for their talents such as: healer/helper, creative channels like arts and crafts, or being the victim/martyr.

Chapter 2

LOVE AND ROMANCE

THE SPREADS IN THIS CHAPTER ARE ALL BASED
on love and romance. Everyone is interested in new
relationships, romantic involvements, and commit-
ments of some sort. There is much excitement at the
prospect of meeting someone new!

The spreads in this chapter are:

> A New Lover
>
> A Romantic Attraction
>
> Lover's Spread
>
> Magical Love
>
> Guide for Lovers

All the spreads have readings that explain them
except for the last, Guide for Lovers. Test your own
abilities on this spread and see how well you do! If
you have studied the "Key Words" and memorized
them, you should have no problem doing the reading.

A NEW LOVER

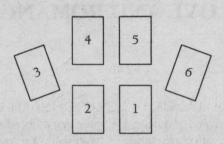

1. Will there be a new relationship for me soon?
2. What astrological sign will this person be?
3. Will we be compatible?
4. Will this be a lasting relationship?
5. Will this person be my soul mate?
6. What is the outcome of my desire?

A New Lover for Rachel

CARDS IN THE SPREAD

1st   position   Queen of Pentacles
2nd   position   10 of Pentacles
3rd   position   King of Pentacles
4th   position   Temperance
5th   position   7 of Wands (Reversed)
6th   position   Ace of Cups (Reversed)

READING

Question 1: Will there be a new relationship for me soon?

Answer: Queen of Pentacles. This Queen is involved with making money and interested in health and healing. Rachel is an idealist and a perfectionist. She is now enrolled in college where she will meet lots of new people. Rachel is only seventeen, and quite shy. The potential for a relationship during the winter could prove interesting!!

Question 2: What astrological sign will this person be?

Answer: 10 of Pentacles. All Pentacles refer to Earth signs. Rachel is a Capricorn and perhaps she will attract an Earth sign into her life!

Question 3: Will we be compatible?

Answer: King of Pentacles. This is an Earth sign (Taurus). They can be compatible as long as he is financially stable. Rachel seems interested in social services and she would like a partner who cares about others. Earth sign relationships can be compatible if they are practical and sharing. Capricorns wish for success and can push their partners to attain their own goals.

Question 4: Will this be a lasting relationship?

Answer: Temperance. Rachel needs self-control, harmony, and balance. This card is ruled by Sagittarius, which is a freedom sign. They rarely stay in relationships for long periods of time. Learning about partners or mates takes time. Take a trip now!

Question 5: Will this person be my soul mate?

Answer: 7 of Wands (Reversed). This is the first reversed card in this spread. This card shows no victory and feeling socially inferior or incompetent. Path unclear for the future. Rachel may be disappointed with this individual and find he is not what she thought he was.

Question 6: What is the outcome of my desire?

Answer: Ace of Cups (Reversed). Rachel does not foresee any new beginnings in love relationships for herself. There is emotional instability and she feels drained. She is ready to begin her first semester in college and feels uncertain. Rachel is seventeen and talks of waiting a year before entering college.

Comment: Rachel's parents insist she go to school or work. She does not drive, so work may be difficult. Rachel is a Capricorn and she needs a career focus. A good education can teach her to become financially independent. It is hard for young adults to make decisions with so many possibilities.

A New Lover for Denny

CARDS IN THE SPREAD

1st	position	Ace of Pentacles (Reversed)
2nd	position	Knight of Wands
3rd	position	5 of Swords
4th	position	9 of Pentacles (Reversed)
5th	position	Page of Wands
6th	position	10 of Pentacles (Reversed)

READING

Question 1: Will there be a new relationship for me soon?

Answer: Ace of Pentacles (Reversed). This card tells Denny that there will not be any new beginnings especially in money matters. It takes money to go places and do things with a new relationship—now is a time to conserve resources and balance the budget.

Question 2: What astrological sign will this person be?

Answer: Knight of Wands. This Knight, a Leo, brings messages concerning work and social activities. Good news relating to work, a trip, or a change of residence. Relationships or other happy events are coming soon. If the new lover is a Leo, this person will expect attention—to be at center stage. Leos have great expectations, are very creative, and have a great sense of humor.

Question 3: Will we be compatible?

Answer: 5 of Swords. Compatibility means getting along well with others. This card indicates Denny believes in problems and has the desire to overcome others due to his ego needs. This type of rash behavior may be the cause of his lack of friends and relationships. Denny has many desires and this clouds his judgment. Leos are extremely powerful people and Denny should be aware that they can be powerful adversaries.

Question 4: Will this be a lasting relationship?

Answer: 9 of Pentacles (Reversed). Denny seems overly concerned with money matters. When reversed, this card indicates feelings of dependency. It also reflects a lack of wisdom gained through past experiences, loss through friends, or unwise investments. This relationship will last as long as it does not need money to keep it going.

Question 5: Will this person be my soul mate?

Answer: Page of Wands. This Page is a fire sign, as is the Leo from question 2, eager to experience work and social life. They desire freedom, want independence, and love to travel. Action is the aim and goal of this Page. Denny stays close to home, is bound to his job, and will not spend his money without just cause. Perhaps they can teach each other significant experiences to polish each other's character. It is possible they are soul mates!

Question 6: What is the outcome of my desire?

Answer: 10 of Pentacles (Reversed). There will not be any significant change in Denny's financial picture. The only difference will be in his mental attitude. Be happy!

Comment: Half of the cards in this spread are reversed, which shows a negative focus. Denny seems more interested in freedom and money than in a new and lasting relationship. He needs time to grow and mature. Denny's values have not been formed and his sense of responsibility must be activated.

A ROMANTIC ATTRACTION

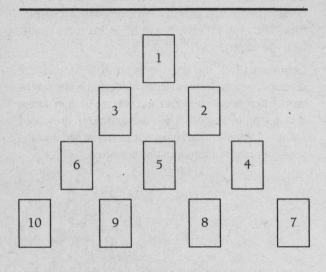

1. What is the attraction?
2. Is this person loving?
3. Can we have fun together?
4. Can we work together and support each other?
5. Will there be sexual compatibility?
6. Will our families get along?
7. Are there religious differences?
8. Will we have problems with power and money?
9. Is this a long-term relationship?
10. What is the outcome?

A Romantic Attraction for Susan

CARDS IN THE SPREAD

1st	position	Sun
2nd	position	Queen of Cups (Reversed)
3rd	position	5 of Wands
4th	position	2 of Wands (Reversed)
5th	position	High Priestess (Reversed)
6th	position	2 of Cups (Reversed)
7th	position	9 of Pentacles (Reversed)
8th	position	4 of Swords
9th	position	9 of Swords
10th	position	King of Cups (Reversed)

READING

Question 1: What is the attraction?

Answer: Sun. Susan sees this man as open, honest, energetic, and youthful. He wants attention, has great expectations (not unreasonable, according to Susan), and wants to be a shining star!

Question 2: Is this person loving?

Answer: Queen of Cups (Reversed). Susan feels he is intense but has an emotional drain regarding women. This Queen can be an implacable enemy—mean and hateful if wronged. This man does not love easily.

Question 3: Can we have fun together?

Answer: 5 of Wands. There could be ego problems between Susan and her new friend. This card indicates a belief held by Susan that she wants her way in work and socially. This could lead to confrontations between Susan and her new relationship. Fighting can be fun but what will the results be for them?

Question 4: Can we work together and support each other?

Answer: 2 of Wands (Reversed). Susan does not know how secure she is in this relationship. She does not know this person very well or for any length of time, however, they had an instant rapport. Unfortunately he lives out of state, which poses problems. Only time will tell!

Question 5: Will there be sexual compatibility?

Answer: High Priestess (Reversed). Susan indicated that it was too early to be involved with this man in a sexually intimate way. She has some fears regarding this relationship and has decided to be cautious. Susan said she did not know when she would see him again.

Question 6: Will our families get along?

Answer: 2 of Cups (Reversed). Susan feels that both families may try to come between her and her new love. This would create an emotional drain and force Susan and her partner to make decisions they are not ready to make. Susan must understand that a good loving relationship is very healthy and worth fighting for, regardless of family interference.

Question 7: Are there religious differences?

Answer: 9 of Pentacles (Reversed). There are no problems with religious beliefs, but Susan feels she lacks wisdom with money and there may be a fear of having to confront that issue. She does not feel like an independently wealthy woman and her new love comes from a very wealthy family.

Question 8: Will we have problems with power and money?

Answer: 4 of Swords. Susan is creating her own problems and troubles. She must realize that her insecurities are driving her to distraction. Now is the time for her to rest, pray, and have faith in herself. If she and her new love are in balance they can work out any problems.

Question 9: Is this a long-term relationship?

Answer: 9 of Swords. Susan is in crisis. She can only see problems and troubles in regard to this relationship. It is almost too good to be true. This man is young, attractive, and he has money! There could be a fear that she does not deserve this wonderful relationship, but why not? If Susan is not careful, it will be over before she has a chance to get involved.

Question 10: What is the outcome?

Answer: King of Cups (Reversed). Susan is feeling drained emotionally and is afraid of losing control. She has a fear of loving and giving her heart away and being hurt in the process. Susan must understand that she must take a chance and believe that it will work.

Comment: Love is the answer to Susan's dilemma. Everyone deserves happiness in life and if money comes with it, all the better! However, since this reading Susan spent time with this person, but the relationship has ended.

A Romantic Attraction for Larry

CARDS IN THE SPREAD

1st	position	3 of Swords
2nd	position	King of Pentacles
3rd	position	Ace of Wands (Reversed)
4th	position	8 of Swords
5th	position	7 of Wands
6th	position	Page of Pentacles
7th	position	6 of Pentacles
8th	position	The Lovers (Reversed)
9th	position	Page of Wands
10th	position	5 of Pentacles

READING

Question 1: What is the attraction?

Answer: 3 of Swords. With this card we see jealousy and problems, and a potential love triangle. Is this romantic attraction a married person, and does Larry enjoy being involved in a relationship he cannot have? Larry must like controversy, but it can lead to serious confrontations and even injury.

Question 2: Is this person loving?

Answer: King of Pentacles. This individual is independent, loving, financially astute, and stubborn. She is not a dependent female but an experienced business person, good with money, and successful. She likes to help others in many different ways.

Question 3: Can we have fun together?

Answer: Ace of Wands (Reversed). At this time Larry is not happy because he does not have much free time to go on trips, begin new projects, or institute new experiences. This is not the time to make new plans for relationships. He needs to focus on work primarily and let his social life rest. If Larry can be light-hearted about this affair then fun can be had with no harm to either party!

Question 4: Can we work together and support each other?

Answer: 8 of Swords. Larry has the strength to cope with this situation, but it may cause more problems than it is worth. He is on unsafe ground and does not want to recognize the danger. Larry should meditate and go within for answers to his questions. He must make his own decisions regarding this relationship.

Question 5: Will there be sexual compatibility?

Answer: 7 of Wands. As long as Larry relies on his mental capacities he can have success no matter what he does. Whether in business or socially, Larry must use his own judgment and express his own ego and willpower. He can have compatibility if that is his desire. Question 2 spoke of the other person as being loving although not dependent. Sex will be a problem if love is missing on Larry's part.

Question 6: Will our families get along?

Answer: Page of Pentacles. If Larry is interested in schooling, has a career focus, or the potential to reach the top of his profession, he will be acceptable to the family of his romantic attraction. He must be ambitious, traditional, and a good provider with a positive attitude about making money. He is not yet sure about this relationship, but the questions still pester him.

Question 7: Are there religious differences?

Answer: 6 of Pentacles. This card indicates that Larry must make some kind of choice regarding finances, being fair, and sharing resources. There could be religious differences between Larry and his love and they must both make adjustments.

Question 8: Will we have problems with power and money?

Answer: Lovers (Reversed). This card shows Larry has a lack of trust in himself and problems involved with commitment or little self-confidence. Larry is apprehensive about making decisions—perhaps he fears making wrong ones. It appears that problems with power and money could lead to alienation. Honesty and trust are essential ingredients in any relationship.

Question 9: Is this a long-term relationship?

Answer: Page of Wands. This Page is eager to experience work and social life. Either Larry or the object of his romantic attraction desire freedom; both are headstrong and independent. They both wish to travel, study foreign cultures, and enjoy life. This relationship may be short and sweet or become a long-term affair that is on and off again and again.

Question 10: What is the outcome?

Answer: 5 of Pentacles. This card indicates that either Larry or his romantic interest may get bogged down with too much work soon. Larry treats money as a god, which is not a healthy attitude and can cripple a person through negative beliefs. This card shows poverty-mindedness without any trust in an inner source. Perhaps neither Larry nor his love feel as supported as they wish to be. The potential for drug use is indicated.

Comment: Any relationship can work if there is love, trust, and a desire to be together. There seems to be many difficulties to overcome in this relationship but with perseverance, it can work out. If she is available, then Larry has a good chance to win the hand of the fair lady. If he cares, nothing will stand in his way!

LOVER'S SPREAD

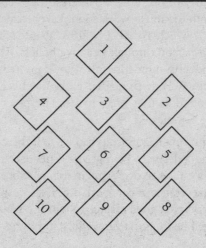

1. Does my lover care for me?
2. Are we compatible?
3. Do we have similar desires and goals?
4. Is my lover faithful and true?
5. Are we attracted to each other sexually only?
6. Will my lover consider marriage?
7. Does my lover have high standards and good values?
8. Can we share our finances and material possessions?
9. Will my lover stay with me or leave?
10. What is the final outcome?

Lover's Spread for Doris

CARDS IN THE SPREAD

1st	position	Temperance
2nd	position	Wheel of Fortune (Reversed)
3rd	position	Page of Cups
4th	position	Fool
5th	position	Knight of Wands
6th	position	High Priestess (Reversed)
7th	position	Hierophant (Reversed)
8th	position	10 of Wands (Reversed)
9th	position	Ace of Cups
10th	position	4 of Cups (Reversed)

READING

Question 1: Does my lover care for me?

Answer: Temperance. Doris must balance her emotional needs and have patience during this difficult period of her life. Temperance shows fire, which is action and energy. She needs to slow down and enjoy her life, which is not easy for a fire sign (she is a Leo). Doris' lover cares for her, but is not ready to commit to a lasting relationship.

Question 2: Are we compatible?

Answer: Wheel of Fortune (Reversed). There are no changes in Doris' relationship. She should not gamble or take any risks with her lover, instead just go with the flow. Doris desires to be admired and loved, and her lover gives her what she needs when they are together.

Question 3: Do we have similar desires and goals?

Answer: Page of Cups. Both Doris and her lover are

very sensitive, creative, and have psychic ability. This Page can bring good news regarding love relationships, parties, births, and marriages (not necessarily one's own). The card can indicate that both Doris and her lover are immature, illusory, and possibly troubled with liquor or drug problems. Their goals may not coincide.

Question 4: Is my lover faithful and true?

Answer: Fool. Doris' lover wants adventure, new experiences, and being out and about. Since there is no commitment, her lover is free to do as he pleases.

Question 5: Are we attracted to each other sexually only?

Answer: Knight of Wands. The Knight brings information concerning work and social activities. There are plans for a trip or change of residence. Doris is trying to do both—she is buying a condo and travels for her job. These activities do not give her much time to indulge in building a future for herself and her lover.

Question 6: Will my lover consider marriage?

Answer: High Priestess (Reversed). Doris does not think so. She feels he has a closed mind, fears commitment, and lacks self-confidence. He may not want an overly intelligent female in his life.

Question 7: Does my lover have high standards and good values?

Answer: Hierophant (Reversed). Doris thinks her lover is a pleasure seeker, indulgent, and materialistic. He enjoys sexual pleasures and being with Doris but does not seem to want a closer relationship. The Hierophant reversed shows a rebellious person who does not abide by the rules. If his standards and values are not high, Doris must re-evaluate this relationship.

Question 8: Can we share our finances and material possessions?

Answer: 10 of Wands (Reversed). Doris feels burdened at this time with her own needs, including trying to buy a condo for herself. She may not be keen on sharing her resources without a show of good faith from her lover.

Question 9: Will my lover stay with me or leave?

Answer: Ace of Cups. This card tells Doris that she will have new beginnings in her love life. She will have a new residence within the year, happiness and pleasure will follow! This card also relates to new emotional involvements. Perhaps this lover will depart from Doris' life?

Question 10: What is the final outcome?

Answer: 4 of Cups (Reversed). Doris is not realizing how she feels emotionally. She is disappointed in her love relationship; she has great expectations but fears commitment or rejection. She has been married and divorced and does not wish to repeat the experience.

Comment: With all the reversed cards in this spread, it does not seem likely that this relationship will continue and result in marriage. This agrees with Doris' thinking, but that can change in an instant—perhaps her real love is waiting in the wings? Since this reading, Doris has moved to Australia with a new love!

Lover's Spread for Suzanne

CARDS IN THE SPREAD

1st	position	8 of Swords (Reversed)
2nd	position	The Tower (Reversed)
3rd	position	9 of Cups
4th	position	The Hierophant (Reversed)
5th	position	Knight of Wands
6th	position	7 of Pentacles (Reversed)
7th	position	Queen of Wands (Reversed)
8th	position	Judgment (Reversed)
9th	position	6 of Swords
10th	position	8 of Wands

READING

Question 1: Does my lover care for me?

Answer: 8 of Swords (Reversed). This card indicates that Suzanne should let go of this unhealthy relationship. Her lover does not have the stamina to maintain a good love relationship—or perhaps they are in ill health? This card may also show a lack of confidence or faith in herself. There are problems in this relationship that must be addressed soon.

Question 2: Are we compatible?

Answer: The Tower (Reversed). She must learn to evaluate her past experiences to see if she has repeated the same type of relationship, but she refuses to give up her old habit patterns. The focus is on sexuality, jealousy, and resentment which could refer to her personally or her lover. There may be financial problems.

Question 3: Do we have similar desires and goals?

Answer: 9 of Cups. This is the wish card and it is upright—indicating that the wish Suzanne made at the beginning of the reading will be granted. She must use her intuition and wisdom gained through experience at this time. She feels they both want the same things and are working toward their goals.

Question 4: Is my lover faithful and true?

Answer: The Hierophant (Reversed). This card in a reversed position indicates that her lover may be a pleasure seeker, indulgent, and materialistic, as well as intolerant and judgmental. This person may have a closed mind and have little faith in self. This lover may not be ready for a serious commitment.

Question 5: Are we attracted to each other sexually only?

Answer: Knight of Wands. This card infers that ego needs are the most important element in this relationship. There are messages coming to Suzanne regarding work and social activities. Suzanne has good news in store for her relating to a trip, a possible change of residence or news of a marriage. Perhaps her own?

Question 6: Will my lover consider marriage?

Answer: 7 of Pentacles (Reversed). This card shows an uncertain path to money and success not assured. At this time, her lover is probably not willing to commit to a marriage. There may be more health problems, both Suzanne and her lover may feel frustration, anxiety, and a lack of confidence.

Question 7: Does my lover have high standards and good values?

Answer: Queen of Wands (Reversed). This card refers to the ego and the need for attention, praise, and applause. Suzanne's lover may have high standards for himself and a sense of values that refer to him alone. This lover has great expectations that must be fulfilled by the other person. Suzanne may have a difficult time living up to his needs and expectations.

Question 8: Can we share our finances and material possessions?

Answer: Judgment (Reversed). Either Suzanne or her lover is focused on material gain. There is a lack of judgment regarding each other and the inability to see truth in this relationship. They need to discuss their financial status honestly and learn to trust each other before there is any talk about commitment.

Question 9: Will my lover stay with me or leave?

Answer: 6 of Swords. There is a temptation to run away from problems and Suzanne's lover is caught in a dilemma. The lover may not feel the relationship is worthwhile, nor does he desire a commitment now. Perhaps Suzanne or her lover should take a trip and try to see if "absence makes the heart grow fonder."

Question 10: What is the final outcome?

Answer: 8 of Wands. Suzanne has the strength to work and have social activities. She can overcome any problems if she desires.

Comment: This relationship has many problems but they are not insurmountable. Love will find a way! Communicate.

MAGICAL LOVE

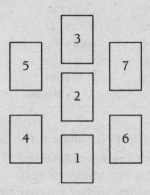

---

1. Will I ever find my true love?
2. Will I feel safe and secure with this person?
3. Is marriage a potential for me?
4. Will this new love be similar to my past lovers?
5. Will commitment be possible with this new love?
6. Can the magic last between us?
7. What can I do to make this person part of my life?

Magical Love for Denis

CARDS IN THE SPREAD

1st	position	High Priestess (Reversed)
2nd	position	Sun (Reversed)
3rd	position	3 of Pentacles
4th	position	9 of Cups (Reversed)
5th	position	6 of Cups (Reversed)
6th	position	7 of Pentacles
7th	position	Page of Pentacles (Reversed)

READING

Question 1: Will I ever find my true love?

Answer: High Priestess (Reversed). Denis says he does not know the meaning of life or how to make a good relationship. He has a closed mind and fixed attitude. His parents were divorced when he was very young and now he fears a commitment. Denis could be too critical or over-analytical in his relations with others. True love sees only perfection in the loved one!

Question 2: Will I feel safe and secure with this person?

Answer: Sun (Reversed). Denis will feel safe and secure with anyone if he feels that way about himself. He lacks courage and may have low self-esteem, which does not help his needs. Denis must learn to accept himself first. He is a handsome young man and must have confidence in himself, be open and honest, and not fear rejection. Reversed, this card speaks of little ego and less energy—something that can be overcome.

Question 3: Is marriage a potential for me?

Answer: 3 of Pentacles. The 3 of Pentacles refers to the master craftsman—a person successful in their chosen field and very creative. Denis makes money because he is good in his work. His talents will eventually bring him rich rewards, but he wants everything now. This card indicates that Denis wants a partner who has creative talents and can make money. Marriage is more than a potential if he can find a female who supports herself and shares her resources with him.

Question 4: Will this new love be similar to my past lovers?

Answer: 9 of Cups (Reversed). Denis is a Scorpio and very intense regarding his desires, but if he lacks the wisdom of his experiences in love, then he is doomed to repeat his past. If he is not aware of his emotional drains, he will bring the same type of relationship into his life. Without new information or the refusal to evaluate past experiences, repeat performances are inevitable in every area of a person's life. It is time to change beliefs.

Question 5: Will commitment be possible with this new love?

Answer: 6 of Cups (Reversed). This card reversed warns to be careful, as someone is making decisions for you. If Denis is not making his own choices with this new love, he will feel trapped. There is a potential for this experience to be emotionally draining for Denis. Commitment is possible but is it practical?

Question 6: Can the magic last between us?

Answer: 7 of Pentacles. The path to magic is financial for Denis. His mental focus is on financial responsibilities and feeling secure—having money in the bank. Life is magic, but people tend to look for flaws, making the magic disappear. If Denis loves himself and accepts himself, he can make a wonderful relationship and the magic could last forever.

Question 7: What can I do to make this person part of my life?

Answer: Page of Pentacles (Reversed). This Page is not interested in schooling, setting goals, or earning money. It indicates that Denis may want the easy life, preferring to not work too hard, and resenting authority figures. If Denis wants a lasting relationship he must make some changes in his thinking. By paying attention to his thinking and beliefs, he can change his life. Remember—what you believe, you manifest. This is true for everyone.

Comment: Denis has had several relationships but none lasting. His parents were divorced and his early conditioning did not give him a feeling of security. Denis is thirty and does not feel successful. He has returned to school (medical) since this reading and hopes to become a physician's assistant. He has also begun a new relationship. Three cheers for Denis!

Magical Love for Adele

CARDS IN THE SPREAD

1st   position   Hanged Man
2nd position   5 of Pentacles (Reversed)
3rd   position   Ace of Wands
4th   position   10 of Pentacles
5th   position   Ace of Pentacles (Reversed)
6th   position   Hierophant
7th   position   Queen of Swords (Reversed)

READING

Question 1: Will I ever find my true love?

Answer: Hanged Man. Adele feels she has been sacrificed to the will and desires of others. She must learn to have faith in herself and stop living in fantasy. She will find true love after she learns to love herself. She must also learn to meditate.

Question 2: Will I feel safe and secure with this person?

Answer: 5 of Pentacles (Reversed). Adele has not made money her god. She is surrounded by ambitious family members and wishes to live her life differently. At seventeen, she may feel she needs to get a job and be independent. If Adele enters a relationship, she will accept this person on her terms, not based on what others want her to do. Adele is beginning to have faith in her own talents and also herself. Feeling secure must come from within oneself. She is a Leo with a mind of her own.

Question 3: Is marriage a potential for me?

Answer: Ace of Wands. Marriage is always a potential for anyone who desires it. Adele is slated to have new beginnings in work and socially. There will be new contacts for her and perhaps some new opportunities. Adele's parents are divorced and both have remarried. She may crave excitement and bring someone new into her life, but love and marriage may take time.

Question 4: Will this new love be similar to my past lovers?

Answer: 10 of Pentacles. Adele remarked that she was too young to have had a past lover. She is waiting to see the type of relationship she will attract. This card indicates a change of fortune and foretells better times ahead for her.

Question 5: Will commitment be possible with this new love?

Answer: Ace of Pentacles (Reversed). The potential of this first relationship ending in commitment is not likely. The card signifies that Adele must conserve her resources during this period. Perhaps her first love will not have resources of his own and must finish school before accepting a commitment.

Question 6: Can the magic last between us?

Answer: Hierophant. This card indicates Adele is looking for a teacher. At this time, Adele should seek an inner teacher and meditate—going within herself to find answers to her problems. Her beliefs may be creating negative experiences in her life. She longs for approval and resents authority. The magic can last if she is not criticized in this relationship.

Question 7: What can I do to make this person part of my life?

Answer: Queen of Swords (Reversed). Adele's mother is a Libra and so is this card. Adele's mother has had a dramatic effect on her. Mom is successful and works hard. Adele has two sisters and sibling rivalry may be part of the problem. Adele has lived with her dad and stepmother the last few years and is not very happy with this arrangement. The Queen of Swords reversed shows that the person does not wish to be alone, they prefer to be in relationships. At this point, Adele must meet someone before she needs to worry about how to make them a part of her life. She does not want to stay single for long even though she is only seventeen.

Comment: Adele insisted on doing this particular reading. She is not involved with anyone but seems to be in a hurry to find someone who will love her and rescue her from her family. She has had a rough childhood and had problems as a teenager. Time will tell whether she changes her thinking and beliefs and decides to have a good life in spite of her past experiences. As of early 1997, Adele has an apartment with a female roommate. She works and goes to college. She's a non-conformist, through dress, no hair, and rings in her ears, nose and tongue.

Magical Love for Julie

CARDS IN THE SPREAD

1st	position	Page of Wands
2nd	position	World (Reversed)
3rd	position	High Priestess
4th	position	5 of Pentacles
5th	position	7 of Pentacles
6th	position	King of Swords
7th	position	Queen of Pentacles

READING

Question 1: Will I ever find my true love?

Answer: Page of Wands. Julie is a Sagittarius and this card is her. She is a freedom lover, loves new experiences, is independent, and desires to travel. Perhaps Julie does not want a permanent relationship due to her need for freedom. She disclosed her desire to find a younger man and I agreed with her.

Question 2: Will I feel safe and secure with this person?

Answer: The World (Reversed). No. The financial picture does not look promising. Julie will not feel supported and this will create problems.

Question 3: Is marriage a potential for me?

Answer: High Priestess. The High Priestess says Julie is intelligent and has the answers within herself. She will know whether a relationship is right.

Question 4: Will this new love be similar to my past lovers?

Answer: 5 of Pentacles. The 5 of Pentacles infers the lover desires money and may be into liquor or drugs. She feels this person is crippled in some way which may relate to financial aspirations. The belief in money rather than faith in the self is not positive. Julie must ask herself if past relationships had money problems.

Question 5: Will commitment be possible with this new lover?

Answer: 7 of Pentacles. The 7 of Pentacles reveals Julie's desire to be in charge of her own money and its dispersal. She works for her money and does not want anyone to tell her what to do with it. She has her own financial path. The seven does not indicate commitment unless it is on Julie's terms.

Question 6: Can the magic last between us?

Answer: King of Swords. This card may refer to legal proceedings or her lover (Gemini). Julie desires a partner with career potential and intelligence. The magic seems to be in the finances rather than in love. A prenuptial agreement can remove the magic.

Question 7: What can I do to make this person a part of my life?

Answer: Queen of Pentacles. With the Queen of Pentacles, sex and money seem to be the solution. This is the card of pregnant money or a child. Julie feels if she has more money, she will attract a lover, but she doesn't want to share resources or be dependent. This is a dilemma!

Comment: Look at your dependency needs. Learn to trust yourself and decide to have a happy life.

GUIDE FOR LOVERS

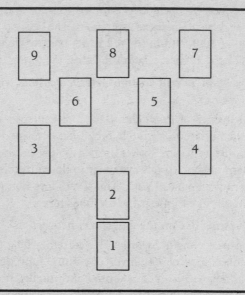

1. What type of mate am I seeking?
2. Will this person be nurturing, loving, and supportive?
3. Will communication be a problem between us?
4. Does this person work or have a career?
5. Will our attraction be sexual, emotional, or mental?
6. Are we mature enough to have a serious relationship?
7. Will our religious beliefs be compatible?
8. What financial difficulties might there be?
9. What can I do to bring this person into my life?

Chapter 3

HOME AND FAMILY ISSUES

THE SPREADS IN THIS CHAPTER ARE:

Family Problems

Health Spread

A Thief in the Home

Lost Articles Spread

Family issues are important to each person and "Family Problems" can show how matters began and how they have escalated. The "Health Spread" can inform the individual how they are punishing themselves due to long-held beliefs.

"A Thief in the Home" came about during a conversation with a friend who was very upset after being robbed and needed to release his anger. It was then the spread was born! Inspiration comes from many directions and we must be alert to this potential.

The final spread in this chapter is "Lost Article." It does not have a sample reading, but is fairly clear. The questions may jog the querent's memory, reminding them where they placed the item.

Remember, each spread is serious to the querent. As a reader, you must try to lighten their burdens by providing pertinent information they can use.

FAMILY PROBLEMS

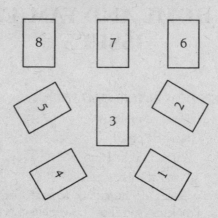

1. Who is primarily involved with the problem?
2. What is the conflict regarding your security or safety?
3. How is dysfunctional behavior an issue in the problem?
4. Has this person had similar problems in the past?
5. What steps must be taken to resolve this matter?
6. Are there situations you should avoid?
7. What effect do these problems have on your health?
8. What are the end results?

Family Problems for Tom

CARDS IN THE SPREAD

1st	position	10 of Wands (Reversed)
2nd	position	9 of Pentacles (Reversed)
3rd	position	World
4th	position	7 of Swords
5th	position	9 of Wands
6th	position	8 of Swords
7th	position	8 of Cups (Reversed)
8th	position	6 of Wands (Reversed)

READING

Question 1: Who is primarily involved with the problem?

Answer: 10 of Wands (Reversed). Tom feels he is carrying heavy burdens at work and socially. All the people involved are family and Tom thinks he is trapped in the situation. He does not see any possibility for changes at the present time. He spoke of the obstacles to any plans that are frustrating him.

Question 2: What is the conflict regarding your security or safety?

Answer: 9 of Pentacles (Reversed). Tom is realizing his lack of wisdom in money matters. He does not think the family backs him in his decisions but feels dependent now that his money is tied up in the family business.

Question 3: How is dysfunctional behavior an issue in the problem?

Answer: World. One member of the family has back problems, which is creating emotional turmoil, and another is not carrying a fair share of the responsibilities, according to Tom. But with the World card here, it is indicated that success in all endeavors will be the outcome. Tom has support from his inner resources and can maintain balance through any crisis.

Question 4: *Has this person had similar problems in the past?*

Answer: 7 of Swords. Tom remarked that problems are part of the picture. The individual with back problems has had them before, and the other person was not interested in tying himself down to work. The situation may be temporary and can change quickly. Tom feels cheated or that others are stealing from him.

Question 5: *What steps must be taken to resolve this matter?*

Answer: 9 of Wands. Tom needs to use wisdom at work and socially. Tom must use fair tactics and achieve his goals through intelligence while learning to protect himself and his interests at work and socially.

Question 6: *Are there situations you should avoid?*

Answer: 8 of Swords. There is no way for Tom to avoid his problems. He feels in bondage and on unsafe ground, but he will get his footing soon. Fortunately he has the strength to cope with his situation and should look within for answers. Tom must maintain his health in order to keep the business flourishing.

Question 7: What effect do these problems have on your health?

Answer: 8 of Cups (Reversed). Tom cannot leave this situation. At this time, he feels all right but the emotional drain will have an effect eventually.

Question 8: What are the end results?

Answer: 6 of Wands (Reversed). Tom must take care not to make unwise choices due to his frustrations. Avoiding setbacks by taking right actions is important, and negative use of energy will create worse problems. Tom should be prepared for delays and frustrations until he can set new moves in motion.

Comment: It is difficult to separate a family involved with business—everyone must share the blame when problems arise. In this case, the family issues are tied to a business in which these people are involved. Matters have become so intense that the health of at least one member and the emotional body of another have been affected. The only solution is to "wait and see" what will happen, otherwise the financial aspect of the business will suffer and everyone will lose.

Family Problems for Gerry

CARDS IN THE SPREAD

1st	position	7 of Cups (Reversed)
2nd	position	The Fool (Reversed)
3rd	position	9 of Cups
4th	position	King of Pentacles (Reversed)
5th	position	Ace of Cups (Reversed)
6th	position	Knight of Swords (Reversed)
7th	position	Page of Pentacles
8th	position	2 of Wands (Reversed)

READING

Question 1: Who is primarily involved with the problem?

Answer: 7 of Cups (Reversed). Gerry feels negative because her love and emotional needs are not being fulfilled. She is not using her abilities for creative visualization, which might help her get over this negativity. There is a potential for drugs or liquor that could be part of the problem in the family.

Question 2: What is the conflict regarding your security or safety?

Answer: The Fool (Reversed). Gerry does not want to do anything foolish, but she is anxious about her financial status and her health. Staying in a negative situation is not usually positive.

Question 3: How is dysfunctional behavior an issue in the problem?

Answer: 9 of Cups. This is the wish card and when it is

up, it means the person will get their wish. Gerry was pleased to hear this. Gerry is gaining wisdom through her experiences, and this can help her in future relationships. She is also gaining confidence in her emotional life. If drugs or liquor are involved, she will know how to handle the experience without feeling like a victim. As they say, "experience is the best teacher."

Question 4: Has this person had similar problems in the past?

Answer: King of Pentacles (Reversed). This King indicates someone who is lazy, selfish, a speculator, and impractical with money. This person may be dishonest and can use shady business practices. Gerry sees this individual in her family as sensual, loving luxury, and desiring pleasure. This person is not willing to share resources, and Gerry feels unloved. This individual will not change and Gerry must make her own decisions about what is best for her.

Question 5: What steps must be taken to resolve this matter?

Answer: Ace of Cups (Reversed). Gerry does not see any new beginnings in her life at this time. She is having an emotional drain and her love is turning into bitterness. Gerry will soon need to make some decisions, discuss the matter openly with this individual, or leave. Confrontation is sometimes the only way to resolve a situation.

Question 6: Are there situations you should avoid?

Answer: Knight of Swords (Reversed). This Knight

carries news of problems and troubles. This message, which is an unreliable source of information, may or may not concern Gerry. She must avoid becoming depressed or feeling like a victim. She can always make a decision to leave the situation and go out on her own, away from the family. The ties that bind can be severed!

Question 7: What effect do these problems have on your health?

Answer: Page of Pentacles. This Page refers to the student. By going to school and getting a better education, Gerry's life can improve and her health will be good. Now is the time for a change in focus to something positive, which will also keep her healthy.

Question 8: What are the end results?

Answer: 2 of Wands (Reversed). Gerry does not have enough confidence in herself. She needs more education—she feels she doesn't know her work or her place in society. Gerry is afraid of failure and perhaps needs to return to her family, but she does not want that to happen. This indicated that Gerry has a closed mind, is critical, and has little ambition.

Comment: Looking at the cards in this spread and seeing that six cards are reversed lets the reader understand that the person has a negative outlook on life. There is fear and guilt within this mind, which causes Gerry to be overly cautious in her actions. Lack of self-confidence and an inferiority complex are playing large parts in her life, as well. The big question is "when will Gerry learn to enjoy life and be happy?" Perhaps the reading will give her some insight into her thinking and she will change her life.

HEALTH SPREAD

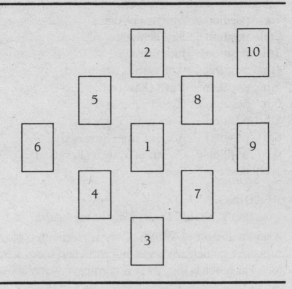

1. Should I worry about my health?
2. How do I overcome my fears?
3. Will I ever be happy?
4. Past feelings of guilt and resentment?
5. Past feelings of depression or unhappiness?
6. Past health problems?
7. Do I need formal medical attention?
8. Will my physical health affect my financial health?
9. Will spiritual awareness aid in overcoming any health problem?
10. Outcome?

Health Spread for Cory

CARDS IN THE SPREAD

1st	position	Knight of Wands
2nd	position	3 of Pentacles
3rd	position	Judgment
4th	position	9 of Wands (Reversed)
5th	position	Devil (Reversed)
6th	position	High Priestess
7th	position	8 of Cups (Reversed)
8th	position	Ace of Cups (Reversed)
9th	position	Queen of Wands (Reversed)
10th	position	Star

READING

Question 1: Should I worry about my health?

Answer: Knight of Wands. Cory is receiving positive messages, particularly regarding work and social activities. His health is fine, there is nothing to worry about.

Question 2: How do I overcome my fears?

Answer: 3 of Pentacles. This is the card of the master craftsman who makes money because he is good at what he does. Think about your worth when it comes to earning money and don't be swayed. The number 3 refers to creative visualization, which can be used to overcome any problem or fear.

Question 3: Will I ever be happy?

Answer: Judgment. It will be up to Cory to make himself happy. Awareness and understanding must be used, and being in touch with the inner self is important. As Cory put it, "Arise and come from the grave of ignorance."

Question 4: Past feelings of guilt and resentment?

Answer: 9 of Wands (Reversed). Cory says he did not use wisdom through his experience at work and is now suing his boss for wrongful termination. The allegations have created some health problems for Cory, but nothing long-lasting. He did not protect himself at work with his employers, and there was a great deal of jealousy with the other staff. Cory had many steady customers who appreciated his dedication to service.

Question 5: Past feelings of depression or unhappiness?

Answer: The Devil (Reversed). Cory is not willing to chain himself to the devil for materialistic gain. Cory has been in spiritual work most of his life and when negative experiences happen he is shocked. He has become unhappy due to his character being maligned. Some of his friends have depressed him also. Crisis periods can relieve boredom and Cory needed a change whether he was aware of it or not.

Question 6: Past health problems?

Answer: High Priestess. The High Priestess knows all about health and everything else. Cory has good health with no history of major illness. Because he believes in health as a natural outcome of life, he does not bring negative thoughts about health into his life.

Question 7: Do I need formal medical attention?

Answer: 8 of Cups (Reversed). When Cory doesn't have the strength to turn his back on an emotional situation, he takes an aspirin. He told me during the reading that he drinks lightly to combat an over-abundance of sensitive feelings. He is very open psychically and tends to "pick up" on other people's thoughts. He claims that meditation helps him overcome negativity around him.

Question 8: Will my physical health affect my financial health?

Answer: Ace of Cups (Reversed). This card shows an emotional drain and no new beginnings. Cory does not like inactivity! He will initiate new experiences, including financial ones, through his will. Being spiritually aware, Cory knows only "wellness" and is focused on this attitude.

Question 9: Will spiritual awareness aid in overcoming any health problem?

Answer: Queen of Wands (Reversed). Cory has a need for ego-recognition and wants attention. He is an Aquarian and this is a Leo card. (These signs are the opposites of each other.) His spiritual understanding keeps him from going overboard in his desires and his attitude keeps his health problems to a minimum.

Question 10: Outcome?

Answer: The Star. Cory must set new goals and "hitch his wagon to a star." He should raise his expectations to create a healthy environment. There is a potential for new directions in Cory's life.

Comment: If Cory continues his spiritual inclinations he will stay healthy. The trial is over and he won! He is going to school for retraining in a new direction.

Health Spread for Lacie

CARDS IN THE SPREAD

1st	position	10 of Cups
2nd	position	Ace of Swords (Reversed)
3rd	position	3 of Cups (Reversed)
4th	position	Temperance (Reversed)
5th	position	Death (Reversed)
6th	position	4 of Pentacles (Reversed)
7th	position	Lovers
8th	position	5 of Swords
9th	position	4 of Swords (Reversed)
10th	position	7 of Swords (Reversed)

READING

Question 1: Should I worry about my health?

Answer: 10 of Cups. Lacie will have major changes in her life regarding love and emotions. She could have joy in the home and with her family. Lacie needs back surgery again (Sword and Pentacle cards can indicate health problems and potential operations). Worry does not solve anything, having faith does.

Question 2: How do I overcome my fears?

Answer: Ace of Swords (Reversed). This card indicates no new beginnings in problems because the old ones are not finished. Lacie has had two back surgeries on the same disc and now needs a third, which is dangerous. Any back problems indicate a lack of support. Lacie is a Capricorn and a very determined person. The way to overcome fear is to have faith in one's inner source.

Question 3: Will I ever be happy?

Answer: 3 of Cups (Reversed). This card shows Lacie does not make herself happy. She is having problems in her relationships, which is creating an emotional drain with the potential for depression and loneliness. Lacie and her husband spend too much time in their business and do not have much time for a social life.

Question 4: Past feelings of guilt and resentment?

Answer: Temperance. Lacie is self-indulgent, restless, and lacking patience. Her desires can lead to waste, loss, or misfortune at this time. Lacie is having back surgery soon and her negative attitude has resulted from past feelings of guilt and resentment.

Question 5: Past feelings of depression or unhappiness?

Answer: Death (Reversed). Lacie is in her sixties and has four children of her own and three children from her second marriage. She has had many years of experience, some not so happy and others quite depressing. By holding on to these negative experiences a person has the tendency to repeat them. If Lacie has a materialistic focus, which is natural to Capricorns, she must decide when she feels secure enough to relax and be happy. Lacie's back problems, which indicate a lack of support from those around her, started in her past and have again recently manifested.

Question 6: Past health problems?

Answer: 4 of Pentacles (Reversed). Lacie has had other medical problems and visited the doctor quite frequently. This card indicates a potential to have health problems due to financial matters, but money problems have not always been the cause of her health afflictions. Lacie has a tendency to have fixed ideas and she is very traditional and does not realize that she is responsible for her condition.

Question 7: Do I need formal medical attention?

Answer. Lovers. This card refers to choices that must be made regarding health matters. She has decided to have a third operation on her back to relieve the pain. Lacie refuses to listen to any alternative suggestions and she must take the responsibility for her actions.

Question 8: Will my physical health affect my financial health?

Answer: 5 of Swords. At this time, Lacie does not have a healthy attitude. She meets the public every day and must wear a happy face. Lacie is in constant pain and this is affecting her adversely. She has had a pleasant demeanor with customers, but that is difficult to maintain with health problems. Lacie's financial affairs will be affected if her operation keeps her bedridden for any length of time. Her husband will need other people to help run their business, which will cut into their profits.

Question 9: Will spiritual awareness aid in overcoming any health problems?

Answer: 4 of Swords (Reversed). This card indicates that Lacie does not realize her problems and troubles. She is burning the candle at both ends. Lacie and her husband say they cannot find good help. Neither of them is interested in spiritual responsibility or information that could change their lives.

Question 10: Outcome?

Answer: 7 of Swords (Reversed). This card reveals that there will be no victory regarding Lacie's problems. The situation is stagnant, and there is potential for jealousy and a lack of love and harmony. Lacie feels she is in an unhappy relationship that may never end. The path she is taking is material, which shows a lack of faith in her inner source. Lacie should re-evaluate her situation and seek answers she may have overlooked. Peace and happiness can happen!

Comment: This situation between Lacie, her son, and her husband must be resolved in order for her health to improve. Lacie and her husband must spend less time working and more time playing. When they straighten out their finances and the time they spend at work, life could be beautiful!

A THIEF IN THE HOME

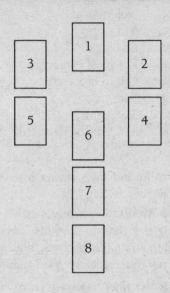

1. Why did I/we attract a thief into the home?
2. Is this thief related to me or my spouse?
3. Is it possible the thief will return?
4. Would an alarm system help in the future?
5. What can I/we do now to change the feelings in the home?
6. What responsibilities did I/we overlook?
7. What did I/we learn from this experience?
8. The outcome?

A Thief in the Home for Stephen

CARDS IN THE SPREAD

1st	position	2 of Wands
2nd	position	6 of Cups
3rd	position	Chariot
4th	position	Knight of Pentacles
5th	position	Queen of Swords
6th	position	Sun
7th	position	3 of Cups
8th	position	8 of Wands (Reversed)

READING

Question 1: Why did I/we attract a thief into the home?

Answer: 2 of Wands. Stephen knows his work and social life. He has the world in his hands and has worked hard to attain this position, but he may fear that he does not deserve all the good coming his way.

Question 2: Is this thief related to me or my spouse?

Answer: 6 of Cups. Stephen thinks the thief is someone he knows and may be distantly related to his wife. This card can indicate someone returning from the past, which could be a relative. He gave this person a key to their home, which was an irresponsible action. Stephen and his wife need to be more discriminating and responsible in the future.

Question 3: Is it possible the thief will return?

Answer: Chariot. This card indicates victory and by controlling desires and guiding himself mentally,

Stephen will be successful. Stephen must meditate and turn to his Higher Self to find out why he attracted the thief in the first place. This can bring positive results to overcome negative experiences.

Question 4: Would an alarm system help in the future?

Answer: Knight of Pentacles. This Knight brings positive messages concerning money. If Stephen and his wife want to install an alarm system the finances will be available. If they continue to give keys away, the alarm system will be useless.

Question 5: What can I/we do now to change the feelings in the home?

Answer: Queen of Swords. This card refers to problems and often indicates a divorced or widowed woman. Stephen is married to a divorced woman and she is now pregnant with their first child. They both feel violated by this thief and are trying to decide what to do. Perhaps the marriage is not as smooth as it should be and both partners are feeling pressured. It is time to evaluate their feelings and be honest with each other.

Question 6: What responsibilities did I/we overlook?

Answer: Sun. Stephen needs confidence in his abilities to make life work out. He must be open to new thoughts and have the courage to carry through. Stephen must seek truth, use his creative talents, and bring success into his life now.

Question 7:What did I/we learn from this experience?

Answer: 3 of Cups. This card refers to pregnancy, a celebration, and good use of creative talents. Stephen has the desire to be happy and enjoy his marriage while he awaits the arrival of his first child. His emotions are positive and he loves his wife. The lesson is learning to think positively and be responsible.

Question 8: The outcome?

Answer: 8 of Wands (Reversed). Stephen lacks strength socially or in his work and feels that the delays and setbacks in his life are keeping him from success. Stephen felt insecure and his thinking was not balanced. He was focused on one person being responsible and was not interested in hearing about the possibility of anyone else being the thief.

Comment: Unfortunately, Stephen has been robbed again since this reading. He is a healer and has worked very hard to be successful in his career. He is in his forties and married for the first time—something he did not expect to happen. As a bonus, they recently had a son. Stephen's life has changed dramatically in less than a year and he now has new responsibilities that may have been overwhelming for him. Stephen will make it through with flying colors if he gives himself the opportunity.

LOST ARTICLES SPREAD

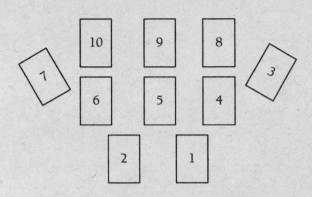

1. What is lost?
2. When did you discover it missing?
3. When was the last time you saw the article?
4. Is it possible you misplaced the article?
5. Should you contact the police?
6. Do you feel guilty or responsible for losing the article?
7. Was the article of sentimental value?
8. Was the article of financial value?
9. Do you have insurance for lost property?
10. Will the article be found soon?

Chapter 4

HIGH FINANCES

IN THIS CHAPTER, ALL THE SPREADS CONCERN a person's finances in one way or another.

The spreads are:

> Business
>
> Career
>
> Lawsuit
>
> Money
>
> Work
>
> Legal Matters

At this writing, all the people involved with these spreads are still trying to resolve their problems. The "Lawsuit" case is still pending, the "Business Spread" querents are doing their best and the individuals in the "Money Spread" are still struggling. Only time will tell if these people manage to overcome their dilemmas.

"Legal Matters 2" does not have a sample reading and you can test your skills with it. There was not another individual available who was involved with a legal battle when the spread was developed.

BUSINESS SPREAD

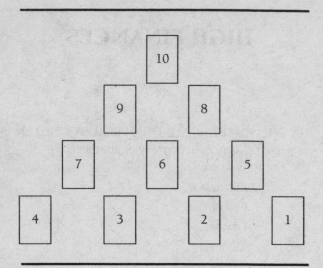

1. Should I begin my own business?
2. Should the business be a partnership?
3. Will the public be receptive to my product?
4. Will the work be difficult?
5. Are there changes I need to make now?
6. Are there responsibilities I have overlooked?
7. Will I be successful?
8. Will I make money through this business?
9. What method of advertising should I use?
10. Final outcome?

Business Spread for Sam

CARDS IN THE SPREAD

1st	position	Queen of Pentacles
2nd	position	Queen of Wands
3rd	position	Page of Swords (Reversed)
4th	position	9 of Cups
5th	position	Hermit
6th	position	7 of Pentacles (Reversed)
7th	position	King of Wands (Reversed)
8th	position	2 of Cups
9th	position	Page of Pentacles
10th	position	The Fool (Reversed)

READING

Question 1: Should I begin my own business?

Answer: Queen of Pentacles. This card is involved with making money and being critical or judgmental. Sam has started his own business, which has been time consuming and demanding. It has already created a health problem for him that he fortunately has overcome.

Question 2: Should the business be a partnership?

Answer: Queen of Wands. Sam has two partners and is not comfortable in this position. One partner might have been fine, but not two. Sam is ambitious and he is seeking success at work and in his social life. His ego needs are involved with this business and he wants admiration and attention.

Question 3: Will the public be receptive to my product?

Answer: Page of Swords (Reversed). This card indicates that Sam does not pay attention to his problems. The public has been receptive to their products and the business is doing well. Sam is anxious and wants success but seems to neglect his personal life.

Question 4: Will the work be difficult?

Answer: 9 of Cups. This is the wish card and when upright in a spread says "Your wish is granted." Sam has enough confidence in his work and is able to put in long hours periodically. There are other people in the business who work full- and part-time. The work itself is not difficult.

Question 5: Are there changes I need to make now?

Answer: The Hermit. Sam owned a business for thirty years, but not in the same field. He has gathered wisdom through that experience and can apply some of that knowledge to his new venture. The partners are enlarging the store to accommodate more customers, so the changes are being made now. Sam is an Aries, and they usually have good ideas, but they don't always stay for the finish.

Question 6: Are there responsibilities I have overlooked?

Answer: 7 of Pentacles (Reversed). This card refers to an uncertain path to money. The number 7 can pertain to legal matters, as well. Through a lack of confidence or feeling little support, this business could suffer. Sam must accept responsibility, but he must also share with the other partners. There can be pettiness and jealousy among the partners now.

Question 7: Will I be successful?

Answer: King of Wands (Reversed). This King is an Aries, as is Sam. If he is being childish, selfish, domineering, and a petty tyrant then the other partners will work against him. Having relationship problems or being overbearing and unyielding will not bring success; working together for the common good will.

Question 8: Will I make money through this business?

Answer: 2 of Cups. Sam knows about his emotions and his ability to love. He understands that a good relationship is healthy. With this knowledge and application, the business, which has shown its potential in the last few years, could prosper.

Question 9: What method of advertising should I use?

Answer: Page of Pentacles. This Page is a Capricorn—the student who goes to school to learn about a career. Capricorn and Aries (Sam) can work well together. Earth and fire. The fire takes action and Earth stays to clean up. Capricorn is financially focused and Aries, as a rule, has great ideas about making money. Sending messages out to schools or places where there are young people is one method. Putting out flyers is another. Hiring young people to work with the customers is a third possibility. Trying different methods to see which works is the solution.

Question 10: Final outcome?

Answer: The Fool (Reversed). This card refers to balance. Sam must balance his pleasures, sexual needs, and any other desires. He must curb his anxieties, have faith in the future, act maturely, and be responsible if he wants his business to succeed. Sam fears being made a fool of, which keeps him unsettled.

Comment: Sam's business is doing very well. The problems seem to stem from relationships. If these three partners do not resolve these issues then chances of success are limited. Life is about people living and working together in harmony. Let's hope these three learn this lesson soon.

Business Spread for Donald

CARDS IN THE SPREAD

1st	position	5 of Cups
2nd	position	10 of Wands
3rd	position	5 of Wands
4th	position	The Tower
5th	position	The World
6th	position	The Star
7th	position	Judgment
8th	position	Wheel of Fortune
9th	position	7 of Wands
10th	position	9 of Wands (Reversed)

READING

Question 1: Should I begin my own business?

Answer: 5 of Cups. Don believes in love but his love is not based in truth. There is the potential for his relationship to suffer due to the strain in his business. Don started his own business several years ago and he spends long hours at his work. He is not sure about keeping the business if it costs him his marriage.

Question 2: Should the business be a partnership?

Answer: 10 of Wands. Perhaps if Don had a partner he could share the burdens at work. With this card there will be major changes in Don's life, which could include new business methods or new opportunities. Don's social life may also become active.

Question 3: Will the public be receptive to my product?

Answer: 5 of Wands. Don believes in his work, but

his ego may cause some problems. He wants his own way and if he decides to take a partner there could be conflicts of will and ego. Don has good products and is proud of his business.

Question 4: Will the work be difficult?

Answer: The Tower. Don must overthrow his false ideas and get rid of his old habit patterns. The work is not difficult at this time, but with the additions Don wants to make it could become so. This would create more strife and discord in his relationship at home and with the rest of his family.

Question 5: Are there changes I need to make now?

Answer: The World. Don would be wise to understand that there is success and attainment in all of his endeavors. If Don knew that he was being supported by his inner source he could relax and allow himself to enjoy the fruits of his labor now. The changes he needs to make: to have more faith in himself, become more balanced, and trust his ability to succeed.

Question 6: Are there responsibilities I have overlooked?

Answer: The Star. The Star card speaks of goals for the future. Perhaps Don needs to set new goals, accept new opportunities, and be optimistic about the future. There are also relationship obligations that must be taken into account. Success at the cost of relationships is not a positive attitude.

Question 7: Will I be successful?

Answer: Judgment. Don has the potential to be very

successful. With new understanding comes more self-confidence. Don's health will improve with awareness of his potential. He may move his residence, take a trip, or just learn to relax. Accepting our inner source and realizing that there is always help will bring joy and happiness into our lives.

Question 8: Will I make money through this business?

Answer: Wheel of Fortune. Now is the time for Don to take a chance, be a gambler, make changes, seek new experiences, and enjoy the family and other relationships. Don must be positive during this period and he will stay healthy and make money.

Question 9: What method of advertising should I use?

Answer: 7 of Wands. This card indicates that Don should rely on his own judgment. He wants to express his ego at work or in social events. Don would prefer a magazine for his ads as well as handbills carried to individuals. Don must trust his own choices in this matter.

Question 10: Final outcome?

Answer: 9 of Wands (Reversed). Don must have more confidence in the business and himself. There could be abuse from outside sources, or even from family. Don may be encountering jealousy and negative feelings from those around him.

Comment: Success is there, but Don must feel he deserves it.

CAREER SPREAD

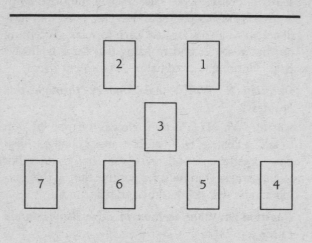

1. Is the career I have chosen what I really want?
2. What steps can I take to improve my career?
3. Are there aspects to my career I cannot change?
4. Do I feel I am doing my best in my career?
5. What changes can I make personally that will help my career?
6. What blocks in my past are affecting my career now?
7. Outcome?

Career Spread for Janice

CARDS IN THE SPREAD

1st	position	The Chariot
2nd	position	5 of Swords
3rd	position	The Moon
4th	position	Knight of Cups
5th	position	9 of Cups (Reversed)
6th	position	High Priestess (Reversed)
7th	position	Emperor

READING

Question 1: Is the career I have chosen what I really want?

Answer: The Chariot. The path Janice took in her career was her choice. She mentally guided herself in the direction of her choice. Janice enjoys her work.

Question 2: What steps can I take to improve my career?

Answer: 5 of Swords. Janice realizes her problems and troubles and is continually bringing more of the same into her life, especially at work. She needs to control her speech and temper for better results. Others may find her aggressive manner difficult to deal with. Janice must learn to balance her ego needs with patience and understanding.

Question 3: Are there aspects to my career I cannot change?

Answer: The Moon. This card indicates progress and attainment cycles. Janice may be living in fantasy and illusion, and her emotions are on overdrive. When an individual works for the government, as Janice does, they are not able to make career changes on a whim, tests must be taken and movement is only possible if positions become open.

Question 4: Do I feel I am doing my best in my career?

Answer: Knight of Cups. Messages of love are coming to Janice that indicate she is doing a good job. She has fifty people working for her in her department and most of them feel she is a good boss and considerate. If she is insecure about doing her best in her job, it is her problem.

Question 5: What changes can I make personally that will help my career?

Answer: 9 of Cups (Reversed). Janice has many wishes concerning her job, but they will not materialize at this time. There is also a lack of wisdom in love which affects her emotional state. Janice needs more faith in herself in dealing with other people. It would be wise of her to love and accept others and herself.

Question 6: What blocks in my past are affecting my career now?

Answer: The High Priestess (Reversed). This card reversed reveals a closed mind and a fear of new information. Janice may not want to know truth, anything about the future, or information regarding herself. She can be stubborn, superficial, and opinionated. Janice did not feel supported by her parents when she was a child and she set out to prove to them that she could be successful—and she is. Her parents are both deceased, but old habit patterns are hard to break. This card, when it appears in a spread for a female, may indicate a need to accept the dependent side of her own nature to create a balance within.

Question 7: Outcome?

Answer: The Emperor. The Emperor is dressed for war, but he is sitting passively. He realizes that he can always fight, but he is going to think before he makes any decisions. This is good advice for Janice. Janice is a mature woman with grown children and she has experienced life. Maturity comes through experience and then applying the knowledge you've gained. The marketplace is usually run by the male population and this is true in Janice's case. For Janice, change will occur only if the boss gets transferred or dies. Janice must enjoy her life and be proud of her position because she has come a long way!

Comment: Janice has done a great deal with her life. She raised her two children without help from her ex-husband, she finished her education while she worked. Now she has a good job as a CPA. She deserves to respect herself—she has mine!

Career Spread for Harvey

CARDS IN THE SPREAD

1st	position	4 of Wands
2nd	position	Judgment
3rd	position	Page of Swords
4th	position	High Priestess (Reversed)
5th	position	Magician (Reversed)
6th	position	Hanged Man
7th	position	3 of Wands

READING

Question 1: Is the career I have chosen what I really want?

Answer: 4 of Wands. This card indicates a fruitful life, marriage, and balance in work and social life. Being an Aries, Harvey does not enjoy being tied down in any one place for long. He feels his choices are not always fruitful or balanced. He has had many job changes in the last year and has not focused on future goals.

Question 2: What steps can I take to improve my career?

Answer: Judgment. Awareness and awakening to truth are both part of the Judgment card. Harvey should learn all he can about his work, then he will reap his rewards. Harvey is impatient, another Aries trait, and wants to experience everything now! He must pay attention to his inner self—understanding does not occur overnight.

Question 3: Are there aspects to my career I cannot change?

Answer: Page of Swords. This card indicates that Harvey will not pay attention to his own problems but will try to solve other people's difficulties. He can be a friend to the world—but at what cost? In order to make any changes in his life he must first work on himself. This Page suggests that Harvey is not as mature as he thinks. Perhaps being more responsible to his own needs will bring maturity. Change is as natural as breathing and will happen regardless of what a person thinks.

Question 4: Do I feel I am doing my best in my career?

Answer: The High Priestess (Reversed). This card infers that Harvey does not know if he is doing his best. He may not be open to new information, tending instead to be closed minded or prejudiced. The High Priestess reversed can indicate fear, guilt, and a refusal to go inside oneself to find truth. Harvey remarked that he felt he was going nowhere—with this attitude, Harvey is not doing his best work due to a lack of self-confidence or self-esteem.

Question 5: What changes can I make personally that will help my career?

Answer: The Magician (Reversed). Harvey feels that there are no new beginnings in any direction and he is frustrated. He would like to force the issue and, through his own will, make events take place. This is not positive at this time. Harvey desires a new job but must wait until something becomes available in his field. One major change he can make—to control his impulsiveness.

Question 6: What blocks in my past are affecting my career now?

Answer: The Hanged Man. The Hanged Man symbolizes the sacrificial lamb. There is a Neptunian attitude surrounding this card which could mean Harvey is into fantasy and illusion. He has old habit patterns he is still dealing with and may be into liquor or drugs, or feeling like a victim or martyr. Meditation— quieting the mind in order to see truth—would help him to get in touch with his blocks.

Question 7: Outcome?

Answer: 3 of Wands. This card is a sign that creative visualization might be an answer. It says "I make or create my work and social activities." Harvey wants a partner in his personal life but does not see this happening in the near future.

Comment: Creative visualization seems to be stressed in this reading and Harvey could benefit from this activity. It is difficult for an Aries person to sit for any length of time, but the rewards could be an incentive. The sooner Harvey gets involved with his own life, the better it will be for him. Since this reading, Harvey has had three different jobs, several girlfriends and has turned thirty.

Career Spread for Linda

CARDS IN THE SPREAD

1st	position	Strength (Reversed)
2nd	position	Knight of Pentacles (Reversed)
3rd	position	4 of Pentacles
4th	position	World (Reversed)
5th	position	9 of Wands
6th	position	High Priestess
7th	position	3 of Wands

READING

Question 1: Is the career I have chosen what I really want?

Answer: Strength (Reversed). Linda feels she is lacking the strength to overcome her difficulties. She may feel lazy, deny herself the good life, and have low self-esteem. Linda is not focused on a career and is in a job she does not like.

Question 2: What steps can I take to improve my career?

Answer: Knight of Pentacles (Reversed). Linda needs to look for a new job while she has her present one. She is waiting for news about money, which she will not receive. If messages do come, they will not contain news about money. The longer Linda waits, the more depressed she will become.

Question 3: Are there aspects to my career I cannot change?

Answer: 4 of Pentacles. Linda must realize her focus

is on money, not her work. She should understand that when you do the work that you love, the money will follow.

Question 4: Do I feel I am doing my best in my career?

Answer: World (Reversed). This card shows no success or material gain at this time. Linda knows she is not doing her best at work. She lacks vision, fears change, is frustrated, and feels she doesn't get the support she craves. Linda is a Pisces, which shows illusion and fantasy as a part of her thinking. She is also overly emotional.

Question 5: What changes can I make personally that will help my career?

Answer: 9 of Wands. Linda has gained knowledge through experience in her work and social life. She also knows how to protect herself in both areas of her life. She must find a job she loves, use her intelligence, and not feel as though she must be on the defensive.

Question 6: What blocks in my past are affecting my career now?

Answer: High Priestess. Linda feels she knows the secrets of the universe. She desires a relationship to be supported, nurtured, and cared for. By discussing her early years as a child, Linda became nervous and upset. It was simple to point out to Linda that she was still laboring under past habit patterns. She has great expectations but she denies herself because she feels she doesn't deserve the best. Linda must forgive herself and others—this will change her life.

Question 7: Outcome?

Answer: 3 of Wands (Reversed). Linda thinks she doesn't make her own work or social life. She is lacking faith in her creative abilities and is not balanced. This card relates to creative visualization and Linda should have no trouble with this. She must make up her mind regarding her career and the direction she wishes to go. With creative visualization, she will reach her goals soon. However Linda must stay away from liquor or drugs, as Pisces are into fantasy and illusion from birth.

Comment: Linda appears to be love-starved. She has little faith or trust in relationships, which is also affecting her work. As a Pisces, she is extremely psychic but not using this talent for her own good. When she realizes that her past experiences and attitudes about them are creating obstacles, she can forgive herself and find success.

LAWSUIT SPREAD

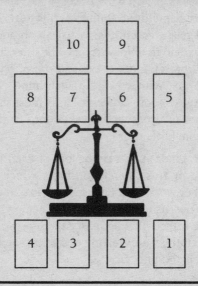

1. What is your concern regarding your case?
2. What is the conflict that is creating your insecurity?
3. Is there a fear of the opposition?
4. Are your motives honest?
5. What changes would you like to make now?
6. Is your lawyer dependable and responsible?
7. Do you visualize yourself winning the case?
8. Will there be financial rewards?
9. How long before the case is settled?
10. Final outcome?

Lawsuit Spread for Kent

CARDS IN THE SPREAD

1st	position	King of Pentacles
2nd	position	3 of Wands
3rd	position	The Fool
4th	position	7 of Swords
5th	position	Ace of Cups
6th	position	7 of Cups
7th	position	Judgment (Reversed)
8th	position	Queen of Wands
9th	position	Empress
10th	position	5 of Swords

READING

Question 1: What is your concern regarding your case?

Answer: King of Pentacles. This is a Taurus card and refers to money. In a sense, Kent feels that his lawyer is in control of the money aspect of his case. He feels she is the power and works independently on his case. Kent is concerned about the settlement and whether he will win the case.

Question 2: What is the conflict that is creating your insecurity?

Answer: 3 of Wands. This card calls for creative visualization. The case has had several postponements and makes Kent nervous. He would like to see it settled and over. The 3 of Wands suggests more communication between Kent and his lawyer. Depression can result if Kent feels ignored and not allowed to know what is happening with his case.

Question 3: Is there a fear of the opposition?

Answer: The Fool. It would be foolish of Kent not to pay attention to the opposition. There are three lawsuits involved with this case. Kent is off to other experiences, but the dog nipping at The Fool's ankles is warning him to pay attention to his case. The opposition is using every delaying tactic possible and Kent must be firm in the knowledge that he will win in the end.

Question 4: Are your motives honest?

Answer: 7 of Swords. Kent feels his path is to clear his good name first. He was wrongfully accused and feels his employer was dishonest. Kent has had his share of problems and troubles for almost two years, and they have affected his mental attitude in negative ways. He realizes his share of the experience and that he helped to create it.

Question 5: What changes would you like to make now?

Answer: Ace of Cups. There are some new beginnings in love and emotions. Through Kent's will, there may be a move to a new home, greater understanding of spiritual work, or some intuitional guidance. Learning new skills is the primary focus for Kent now.

Question 6: Is your lawyer dependable and responsible?

Answer: 7 of Cups. The path of creative visualization. Kent feels his lawyer is very competent. In his mind he sees himself able to do many things when she wins his case. Kent has faith in his lawyer and her ability to get the job done well.

Question 7: Do you visualize yourself winning the case?

Answer: Judgment (Reversed). Due to the last postponement, Kent has become a little unsettled. There is a lack of awareness or he is not paying attention to his inner self. Kent must be faithful to his vision of winning his case and not give up until he has won.

Question 8: Will there be financial rewards?

Answer: Queen of Wands. Yes. This card refers to money coming to Kent, possibly in August, through his lawsuit. He will also get recognition and attention. Kent's social life may also improve.

Question 9: How long before the case is settled?

Answer: The Empress. Part of the case for Kent could be settled in October and the other part may be finished the following May. Kent could help this decision by creative visualization. The Empress makes everything happen through Venus, planet of love. It will be a relief for Kent to get this experience over.

Question 10: Final outcome?

Answer: 5 of Wands. This card shows Kent saying "I believe in my will and my way at work or socially." Faith in his cause is important for Kent at this time. The court will decide many factors of the case, but Kent must pay attention to his part of the drama!

Comment: Creative visualization seems to be the key in this spread, which Kent does regularly. Half the cards refer to other people in his life and their influence can be positive or negative. Kent must pay attention to the details and not allow himself to get distracted. Overall, the spread is positive as most of the cards are in upright positions. Since this reading, Kent has won his lawsuit and is happy!

MONEY SPREAD

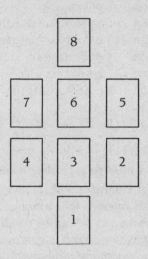

---

1. Concerns regarding money?
2. Desire for financial security now.
3. How can I manifest money to make me happy?
4. Past attitudes regarding money?
5. Issues regarding responsibility for financial well-being?
6. New plans for financial investments or savings?
7. What future plans am I contemplating regarding money?
8. What special abilities do I have for making money?

Money Spread for Robert

CARDS IN THE SPREAD

1st	position	2 of Pentacles
2nd	position	Emperor (Reversed)
3rd	position	4 of Wands (Reversed)
4th	position	4 of Pentacles (Reversed)
5th	position	Page of Pentacles
6th	position	King of Swords (Reversed)
7th	position	Lovers
8th	position	Death (Reversed)

READING

Question 1: Concerns regarding money?

Answer: 2 of Pentacles. Robert says he knows how to balance his money. He is waiting for his financial picture to change so he can be comfortable. Robert invested some money and is concerned because he has not heard good reports about his investment.

Question 2: Desire for financial security now.

Answer: Emperor (Reversed). In his pursuit of financial security, Robert invested in uncertain stocks. Now he is fearful and depressed over his actions. He does not realize that he is materialistic and has made money his god.

Question 3: How can I manifest money to make me happy?

Answer: 4 of Wands (Reversed). Robert does not realize that he is out of balance at work and in his social life. He needs to use creative visualization to bring everything into his life. Robert is not using his mind to good advantage and feels insecure.

Question 4: Past attitudes regarding money?

Answer: 4 of Pentacles (Reversed). Robert did not realize the value of money in the past. He was a spendthrift, gave money to his friends, and saved little for himself. He also had some health problems.

Question 5: Issues regarding responsibility for financial well-being?

Answer: Page of Pentacles. This Page has the desire to earn money and get ahead in his career. Robert is trying to gain his financial goals the easy way but if he is in denial, then he will lose whatever money he has invested. Robert must take responsibility for his thoughts and actions regarding money.

Question 6: New plans for financial investments or savings?

Answer: King of Swords (Reversed). Robert does not have any new plans involving his finances. He is not discriminating when it concerns money and is still waiting to see if this latest investment brings him a windfall.

Question 7: What future plans am I contemplating regarding money?

Answer: Lovers. Robert understands his past habit patterns of denial and wants to change his thinking to bring positive experiences into his life. He must learn to trust his inner self and ask for guidance from this source. Robert has decided not to invest any more money into "get rich quick" schemes.

Question 8: What special abilities do I have for making money?

Answer: Death (Reversed). The Death card is the thirteenth card of the Major Arcana and relates to the twelve disciples and Jesus. Perhaps this relates to spiritual work in Robert's spread, as he is an astrologer with many years of study. Becoming a professional astrologer might be one way he can make money.

Comment: Robert has five cards reversed in this spread which indicates negative thinking on his part. He needs more faith and confidence which can be gained by accepting himself first and using his creative talents to become happy in his life.

Money Spread for Peter

CARDS IN THE SPREAD
1st   position   King of Wands
2nd position   Hierophant
3rd position   Sun (Reversed)
4th   position   King of Cups
5th   position   Lovers (Reversed)
6th   position   3 of Cups
7th   position   4 of Cups
8th   position   Knight of Cups (Reversed)

READING
Question 1: Your concerns regarding money?

Answer: King of Wands. Peter is independent, social, and enjoys entertaining his family. He would like to be financially secure but is on disability pay which limits his funds.

Question 2: Desire for financial security now.

Answer: Hierophant. Peter longs for approval and resents any authority figure or control by others. Meditation may help him to get in touch with his inner guide through which he may be able to remove any blocks relating to his need for security—be it financial, emotional, or mental.

Question 3: How can I manifest money to make me happy?

Answer: Sun (Reversed). Peter has a lack of confidence in himself, yet great expectations from others. This can bring both serious health problems and disappointment to him. Peter must think about prosperity which is a positive attitude and more rewarding.

Question 4: Past attitudes regarding money?

Answer: King of Cups. Peter is a good family man, loving and nurturing, but he needs to feel safe and secure and also share with his family. Peter tends to control his children by being overindulgent and can appear to be a spendthrift.

Question 5: Issues regarding responsibility for financial well-being?

Answer: Lovers (Reversed). Peter does not wish to make decisions about money situations, which could indicate a fear of making mistakes about them. Peter may lack trust in himself or have a closed mind about financial matters.

Question 6: New plans for financial investments or savings?

Answer: 3 of Cups. Peter makes himself happy doing the things he likes best, and financial planning is not on the list. Peter prefers reading, having fun, and making plans to travel with his family. He wants to enjoy his life now!

Question 7: What future plans am I contemplating regarding money?

Answer: 4 of Cups. This card reflects a person out of balance and not noticing that something new is being offered. Peter is caught up in his old habit patterns which must be changed for future growth.

There may be some depression at this time because no plans have been made for a trip or vacation. Peter realizes his love and emotional state but does not feel he can change his circumstances. Perhaps this reading will cause Peter to take notice.

Question 8: What special abilities do I have for making money?

Answer: Knight of Cups (Reversed). This card shows an emotional drain over messages not received. It also shows a potential loss or separation from a loved one. He is a salesman and did well before his surgery. Peter loves to read and he would do well working in a book store. Peter could creatively visualize money coming to him so that he would not need to work.

Comment: There are many people involved in Peter's life, which keeps him busy. The reading reveals that Peter is a sensitive and emotional man. He would like to have more money but is limited in his earning ability. Visualization might be the answer for him.

Money Spread for James

CARDS IN THE SPREAD

1st	position	Ace of Wands
2nd	position	3 of Pentacles (Reversed)
3rd	position	High Priestess (Reversed)
4th	position	Ace of Cups (Reversed)
5th	position	8 of Pentacles (Reversed)
6th	position	Page of Swords
7th	position	8 of Cups (Reversed)
8th	position	Death

READING

Question 1: Concerns regarding money?

Answer: Ace of Wands. James will have new beginnings or opportunities professionally or socially. He must also have some new thoughts about his business in order to be successful. There is new growth potential indicated in this card also.

Question 2: Desire for financial security now.

Answer: 3 of Pentacles (Reversed). James does not feel his creative talents are being used to make more money. His health is good at this time but he had some big problems a short time ago. James is unhappy with one of his partners and cannot see a way to change the situation.

Question 3: How can I manifest money to make me happy?

Answer: High Priestess (Reversed). James has a fixed mental attitude regarding his business and says he doesn't know how to change his situation. James lacks trust in his intuitive abilities. To manifest anything, creative visualization is the answer. Spend ten minutes focused on what you want and have faith that it will occur. Try it!

Question 4: Past attitudes regarding money?

Answer: Ace of Cups (Reversed). James feels emotionally drained. There will be no new beginnings in love, and resentment or anger can indicate a potential for health problems. James had a thriving business for thirty years and money was not a problem. This new business takes too much time, energy, and money.

Question 5: Issues regarding responsibility for financial well-being?

Answer: 8 of Pentacles (Reversed). James does not feel he has the strength to learn new skills or make money. He is very frustrated with one partner and feels that someone is stealing or into criminal activities in the business.

Question 6: New plans for financial investments or savings?

Answer: Page of Swords. James has no new plans financially except to get his business on solid ground. One partner is a young man who has his own agenda, which does not please James. Paying attention to business would please James a lot!

Question 7: What future plans am I contemplating regarding money?

Answer: 8 of Cups (Reversed). James has plans to initiate an expansion program to try to stimulate his business. He is emotionally drained and feeling unloved. There is a lack of strength or drive which may hamper his efforts.

Question 8: What special abilities do I have for making money?

Answer: Death. This card denotes an end to James' situation and a change for the better. New ideas and future plans are healthy. If James can release old resentments and fears and be open to love he can turn the situation into positive avenues of success. James has good ideas but feels that he is being ignored lately, which has depressed him.

Comments: With so many cards reversed, it appears that James is in a negative frame of mind. His wife needs back surgery, which is not a happy event as she also works in their business. It is apparent that James and his wife are not happy due to the materialistic focus they both have.

WORK SPREAD

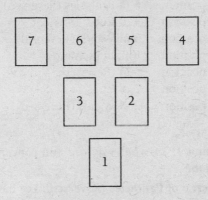

1. In what way are you concerned with your job?
2. Is the conflict beyond your control?
3. Should you communicate your feelings to your boss?
4. Is the work causing physical problems?
5. Will there be changes in the job soon?
6. Should you look for a new job?
7. Final outcome?

Work Spread for Lee Carol

CARDS IN THE SPREAD

1st	position	6 of Pentacles (Reversed)
2nd	position	4 of Cups
3rd	position	3 of Wands (Reversed)
4th	position	Knight of Wands
5th	position	Sun (Reversed)
6th	position	7 of Cups
7th	position	2 of Wands (Reversed)

READING

Question 1: In what way are you concerned with your job?

Answer: 6 of Pentacles (Reversed). Lee has a fear of not earning enough money and is concerned that other people make her financial choices for her. She could be a spendthrift without realizing it.

Question 2: Is the conflict beyond your control?

Answer: 4 of Cups. Lee has been given a new position at work but she has not been told her new salary. Lee has put in a lot of extra time in the last month and was informed that she will not be paid for her efforts. She can't let this depress her and put her out of balance, causing an emotional drain and making her feel used. Unfortunately, there is nothing she can do about the situation.

Question 3: Should you communicate your feelings to your boss?

Answer: 3 of Wands (Reversed). Speaking to her

boss would not be productive. Lee does not have faith in her own abilities and feels that she does not create her own reality. She must learn to creatively visualize what she desires in her life if she wants to change her situation.

Question 4: Is the work causing physical problems?

Answer: Knight of Wands. This Knight brings information concerning work and social activities. This Knight shows activity and energy—he is on the move. There is good news relating to work, planning a trip, or a change of residence. At this time Lee does not have any physical problems due to her job.

Question 5: Will there be changes in the job soon?

Answer: Sun (Reversed). Lee is a teacher and her school is on a year-round calendar. She is on vacation now and is traveling through northern California with her family. When she returns to work, she will have additional work to do as a mentor. She will need to allocate her time differently, creating changes in her daily schedule.

Question 6: Should you look for a new job?

Answer: 7 of Cups. This card refers to creative visualization. Lee must learn to have mental control over her emotions. She loves her students and refuses to contemplate leaving them. Lee understands that nothing stays the same forever, so she will bide her time and stay where she is. Lee is a Taurus, which is a sign of patience, and she has plenty of that!

Question 7: Final outcome?

Answer: 2 of Wands (Reversed). Lee does not wish to take action in her work or social life if she does not have all the answers. She knows that hasty decisions may not be in her best interest. She can be too critical of herself and her abilities—this trip is providing her with breathing space.

Comments: Lee has been a teacher for about ten years and loves what she does. She is a good teacher, bilingual and creative. She is also dedicated to her students. No matter where one works there are always problems and adjustments to be made. Lee needed to get away from all the turmoil going on at her school and this trip was ideal. Spending time with her husband and children will be good for everyone.

Work Spread for Jeff

CARDS IN THE SPREAD

1st	position	Star (Reversed)
2nd	position	Queen of Pentacles
3rd	position	5 of Swords
4th	position	5 of Wands
5th	position	High Priestess
6th	position	6 of Wands (Reversed)
7th	position	7 of Swords

READING

Question 1: In what way are you concerned with your job?

Answer: Star (Reversed). Jeff does not see any future in his job. He is the manager of his company, the highest position he can hold. Jeff must set new goals and use creative visualization to make progress in his life.

Question 2: Is the conflict beyond your control?

Answer: Queen of Pentacles. The owner of Jeff's company is very critical and judgmental. Jeff gets his share of abuse, but the owner gives it to all the help. The owner's wife tries to smooth things over and make life more bearable at work for all concerned. Jeff feels he is doing a good job and would like affirmation from his boss. Jeff has a choice—stay where he is or find another job.

Question 3: Should you communicate your feeling to your boss?

Answer: 5 of Swords (Reversed). Jeff does not

believe in creating problems and troubles. He sees no change in the situation. His boss has his own ideas about running the business and Jeff must obey orders from him. Jeff claims he has tried talking to his boss, but to no avail.

Question 4: Is the work causing physical problems?

Answer: 5 of Wands. Yes. He is having problems with his right knee (the knee relates to career and social standing). Each employee is fighting for recognition at work, and socially he has ego needs that may not be met. Perhaps Jeff needs to evaluate his work situation and make other decisions.

Question 5: Will there be changes in the job soon?

Answer: High Priestess. Jeff said he did not know. Business has been up and down so much lately that he isn't sure. But the High Priestess says he does know. Does this mean that Jeff does not want to see because he might have to make a decision?

Question 6: Should you look for a new job?

Answer: 6 of Wands (Reversed). This card indicates that Jeff should not make a choice at this time or someone else will make his choice for him. Success is not possible at this time but the situation could change.

Question 7: Final outcome?

Answer: 7 of Swords. The 7 of Swords can show positive growth. It also means to have faith in your inner self and ask for guidance. The path Jeff is taking is a mental one, but it is also temporary. He feels cheated in some way or believes that something is being stolen from him. Maybe a new job would be more satisfying for Jeff.

Comment: Jeff feels he is not making progress toward his goal at this time and that he must wait for a better or more clear answer. This analysis may be right, but not if Jeff continues to have physical problems related to his work that are detrimental to his well-being.

Work Spread for Joyce

CARDS IN THE SPREAD

1st	position	Queen of Swords
2nd	position	2 of Wands
3rd	position	9 of Wands (Reversed)
4th	position	9 of Swords (Reversed)
5th	position	6 of Pentacles
6th	position	Ace of Pentacles
7th	position	Lovers

READING

Question 1: In what way are you concerned with your job?

Answer: Queen of Swords. Joyce is a strong-willed woman and determined to make her business successful. She needs a back operation but feels the business is understaffed. Joyce works very hard and desires to be a winner.

Question 2: Is the conflict beyond your control?

Answer: 2 of Wands. Joyce knows what the conflict is in the work area and she has the control in her hands. Problems in the business have manifested a negative health situation for Joyce. She is one of three owners and each feels they know what is best for the business. Joyce must feel somewhat powerless with limited control for her back ailment to have flared up again. Back problems will occur when a person does not feel they are getting the support they deserve.

Question 3: Should you communicate your feelings to your boss?

Answer: 9 of Wands (Reversed). Joyce is not using the wisdom of her experiences in business and feels unprotected. There are two other owners to contend with and each has an ego that must be satisfied. The situation is not healthy and Joyce reflects that unhealthiness.

Question 4: Is the work causing physical problems?

Answer: 9 of Swords (Reversed). It is time to make changes now. Joyce's past experiences have not brought her wisdom or understanding and she is heading toward a crisis. Problems may become insurmountable, but the lessons must be learned. No time for rest and too many bosses are the factors involved in her physical problems. The work is not the culprit, but the mental strain Joyce is laboring under is the cause of her physical problems!

Question 5: Will there be changes in the job soon?

Answer: 6 of Pentacles. Joyce must have an operation on her back. While she is gone, at least two new employees must be hired to replace her. She will have to learn to be fair and share her resources with these new people. There will be changes and Joyce could visualize different ways to make money.

Question 6: Should you look for a new job?

Answer: Ace of Pentacles. Since Joyce owns a share of this business, she is not interested in a "job." One of her business partners is her husband and she must understand that their relationship is based on financial security. They are enlarging their work place and this card indicates that this is a successful move. This card shows new beginnings in money and prosperity and speaks of better health for Joyce.

Question 7: Final outcome?

Answer: Lovers. Joyce must choose what to do with her life. She must use discrimination, be responsible, and have faith that she will make good decisions. Whatever Joyce decides, it will affect her husband and her own family. Removing herself from the combat zone will not solve the problems, only postpone them. She must decide.

Comment: The three bosses of this business are related to each other, and all of them seem to have short fuses. To help their relationship, it would be wise to sell the business. However, it seems this is not possible at this time although the problems are mounting. Getting more help, which would allow Joyce to spend less time working, may defuse the situation.

LEGAL MATTERS SPREAD 2

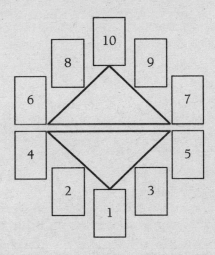

1. What is your concern regarding the legal matter?
2. What is your mental state about this experience?
3. What steps are you taking while you wait for results?
4. Is there a reason for delays or obstacles?
5. How do you feel about your legal counsel?
6. How do you relate to the other person's lawyer?
7. Do you have reliable witnesses?
8. Is your financial position stable?
9. Do you feel supported by your friends and family?
10. Final outcome?

Chapter 5

LIFE'S BIG DECISIONS

THIS GROUP OF FOUR SPREADS CONCERNS some of life's biggest and most important issues. The spreads are:

> Relationship Problems
>
> Marriage
>
> Pregnancy
>
> Divorce Potential

These matters cannot be taken lightly and the reader must be aware of the serious nature of the topic. In many cases, the querent believes that the reader is omnipotent and can "see" the answer to their dilemma.

The last spread in this chapter is "Divorce Potential" and does not have a sample reading. Fortunately, no one came forward with this desire in mind.

The questions in all of the spreads are direct. Each person must do soul-searching in order to find true answers to the questions posed. The Tarot cards have the ability to help resolve their problems if they will allow the truth to shine forth.

RELATIONSHIP PROBLEMS

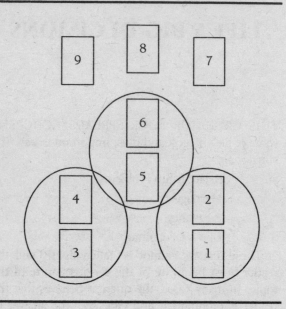

1. What is the problem?
2. The conflict?
3. Did I create the problem?
4. Am I refusing to see my part of the problem?
5. Past experiences with my partner?
6. Are we abusive to each other?
7. Are other people involved with our problem?
8. Are there financial problems affecting our relationship?
9. Will this relationship end?

Relationship Problems for Joanie

CARDS IN THE SPREAD

1st	position	Queen of Pentacles (Reversed)
2nd	position	King of Wands
3rd	position	7 of Wands (Reversed)
4th	position	6 of Swords
5th	position	3 of Swords (Reversed)
6th	position	Hanged Man
7th	position	6 of Wands (Reversed)
8th	position	10 of Swords
9th	position	Page of Wands

READING

Question 1: What is the problem?

Answer: Queen of Pentacles (Reversed). Joanie is a spendthrift and would prefer not to work. She wants to be taken care of and has not found a person to lean on who will support her in the style she wishes.

Question 2: The conflict?

Answer: King of Wands. Joanie has many Aries traits. She wants everything now, to be independent and free. She is ambitious, with executive talents and leadership qualities. Her conflict is in bringing the same type of male into her life who wants her to take care of him and support him. This is very frustrating for her.

Question 3: Did I create the problem?

Answer: 7 of Wands (Reversed). Joanie has an inferiority complex and may feel incompetent. These attitudes can undermine any relationship. Joanie also has a physical and material focus which is not a sound basis for a good relationship. She does not drink, smoke, or indulge in drugs and will not tolerate anyone who does. Due to Joanie's ego needs, if she does not get attention she will end the affair. She understands that she creates her own reality but is determined to find that special person who will fulfill her dreams.

Question 4: Am I refusing to see my part of the problem?

Answer: 6 of Swords. Joanie has been tempted to run away from her problems but she understands that she must stay and face the music in order to advance in life. Joanie had problems with her father when she was a child, and this has colored all her relationships with men. She has begun reading self-help books and wants to realize her part in the situation.

Question 5: Past experiences with my partner?

Answer: 3 of Swords (Reversed). In the past, Joanie believed that she did not create her own problems. She was unhappily married and finally divorced her husband and has not had a long-term relationship since then. Joanie does not respect men due to her negative experiences with her dad.

Question 6: Are we abusive to each other?

Answer: The Hanged Man. Up to this point, Joanie feels that she has been sacrificed to the will of others. She feels in bondage, that no matter what the issue, she will not win. Fantasy and illusion cloud her reasoning and some of her ideas are without substance. Joanie wants something from her relationships but she must learn to let go—in this way she frees herself. No one can abuse her if she won't let them.

Question 7: Are other people involved with our problem?

Answer: 6 of Wands (Reversed). Joanie has siblings and other relatives with whom she is involved. Her dad died recently and she is caught up in an inheritance battle. At this time she wants what she can get from her dad—it may finally resolve her negative feelings about her father and she can get on with her life.

Question 8: Are there financial problems affecting our relationship?

Answer: 10 of Swords. For Joanie there will be big changes in her problems when she receives her inheritance. Many burdens will be lifted and some of her more serious problems will be taken care of. Joanie did not have pressing financial difficulties in her last relationship, but there were emotional ones that undermined it. A new cycle is beginning for her, which can affect her emotionally and bring happier times.

Question 9: Will this relationship end?

Answer: Page of Wands. This Page desires freedom—so did Joanie. The relationship ended soon after the reading.

Comment: Joanie is studying spiritual work in earnest and is now more aware of her attitudes and how they worked against her past relationships. She vows to do things differently in the future.

Relationship Problems for Ann

CARDS IN THE SPREAD

1st	position	3 of Cups (Reversed)
2nd	position	2 of Swords
3rd	position	7 of Wands
4th	position	8 of Pentacles
5th	position	Queen of Cups
6th	position	Emperor (Reversed)
7th	position	6 of Cups
8th	position	The Sun
9th	position	5 of Cups (Reversed)

READING

Question 1: What is the problem?

Answer: 3 of Cups (Reversed). Ann feels she is having an emotional crisis. There is depression, unhappiness, and a lack of creativity in her life. She is also having problems in her relationships.

Question 2: The conflict?

Answer: 2 of Swords. Ann knows her problems and troubles but she doesn't want to see them. She must meditate on her problems to find answers. Ann may need to take action instead of waiting passively for the situation to clear up.

Question 3: Did I create the problem?

Answer: 7 of Wands. Ann should understand that we create our own reality. This path is a mental one and can lead to success and victory professionally.

and socially. Ann needs to take responsibility, not feel superior, and use her ego and will in positive ways.

Question 4: Am I refusing to see my part of the problem?

Answer: 8 of Pentacles. By perseverance in learning new skills and having the strength to cope with all types of experiences, Ann will see that everything ties in together. When we are involved in difficulties, it is often impossible to see solutions!

Question 5: Past experiences with my partner?

Answer: Queen of Cups. This Queen is a Scorpio and associated with love and emotions. Ann is powerful, intuitive, and intense. She is a good friend and a dangerous enemy. She desires to be in control in relationships and is very loyal. Her husband is deceased and she continues to work and stay busy.

Question 6: Are we abusive to each other?

Answer: Emperor (Reversed). Ann is not realizing her potential. She must learn to follow through with her plans, not be lazy or fearful. She must accept the fact that she has to rely on herself and her inner source for guidance. Ann is a widow and independent.

Question 7: Are other people involved with our problem?

Answer: 6 of Cups. This card refers to choices Ann must make regarding love and emotions. She will be tempted to live in the past, but the present is a happier place for her. There are new responsibilities and a potential new relationship. Other people are involved in Ann's life at the present time.

Question 8: Are there financial problems affecting our relationship?

Answer: The Sun. Ann is seeking truth and happiness. There is a potential for financial gain, a trip, and an increase in self-confidence. There are certain limitations, but this card shows no material loss. Health and vitality are assured!

Question 9: Will this relationship end?

Answer: 5 of Cups (Reversed). Ann is still emotionally drained over the loss of her husband. There is some fear of the future and little trust in a relationship. She does not believe in love or romance. If there has been a relationship since her loss, it probably did not last.

Comment. Ann is still young enough to get involved in a good relationship. Companionship is the answer for senior citizens and can give new direction and meaning to life. Now is the time to take a chance!

MARRIAGE SPREAD

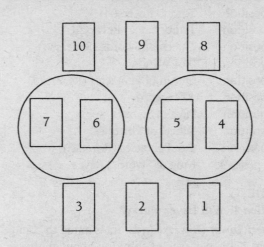

1. Will I ever marry?
2. What kind of mate is compatible?
3. Will we have good methods of communication?
4. Will we both desire a commitment?
5. Will we have similar likes and dislikes?
6. Will this person's family accept me?
7. How shall we find each other?
8. Will we be able to share our financial resources?
9. What can I do while I am waiting for my mate?
10. Outcome?

Marriage Spread for Laura

CARDS IN THE SPREAD

1st position	Tower (Reversed)
2nd position	Temperance (Reversed)
3rd position	Queen of Swords (Reversed)
4th position	5 of Wands
5th position	Queen of Pentacles (Reversed)
6th position	4 of Swords
7th position	Page of Swords
8th position	Wheel of Fortune
9th position	4 of Pentacles (Reversed)
10th position	King of Swords (Reversed)

READING

Question 1: Will I ever marry?

Answer: Tower (Reversed). Laura is afraid to change her old habit patterns of thinking about marriage. She fears losing her freedom; she has had one failed marriage and does not wish to repeat the experience. Potential for a new marriage is now!

Question 2: What kind of mate is compatible?

Answer: Temperance (Reversed). This card shows an imbalance in Laura's emotional life. She is a Gemini and this card is a Sagittarius, the opposite sign. Sagittarius is a freedom lover, one who loves to travel and meet all kinds of people. This would be an ideal situation, although the males Laura has been involved with lately are of the dominant type. Laura admitted that she was afraid of being hurt in love.

Question 3: Will we have good methods of communication?

Answer: Queen of Swords (Reversed). Laura is not open and honest with herself. She would like to be married but fears making a mistake. Laura must communicate this to her new love if she intends to build a lasting relationship.

Question 4: Will we both desire a commitment?

Answer: 5 of Wands. This card relates to strife and disharmony. Laura believes in her own ideas and has the will to see them through, but she believes she must fight to get her ego needs met. She is independent and may decide not to get involved with anyone. She may have a difficult time committing herself at this time.

Question 5: Will we have similar likes and dislikes?

Answer: Queen of Pentacles (Reversed). Laura and her new love have spoken of marriage and children. Laura is not interested in having children and this factor made her more fearful. She wants to enjoy her life and be free to travel. She and her new love have similar tastes, but not in regard to children.

Question 6: Will this person's family accept me?

Answer: 4 of Swords. This card shows an imbalance in Laura's emotional life. Her new love comes from a wealthy family from the East coast and she feels a little uncertain about being welcomed into this family and being hurt in love.

Question 7: How shall we find each other?

Answer: Page of Swords. Laura and her new love

have found each other and they must stop paying attention to others. Listening to her heart's desire will show Laura the way to happiness. Only Laura knows what is best for herself—listening to others can confuse the issue. She can be childish with her fears of losing her freedom by getting married.

Question 8: Will we be able to share our financial resources?

Answer: **Wheel of Fortune.** The Wheel of Fortune says "take a chance, gamble, and travel." Her new love has money of his own and their financial picture looks very bright.

Question 9: What can I do while I am waiting for my mate?

Answer: **4 of Pentacles (Reversed).** Laura must create balance in her finances and health. Money is not the most important issue here. Laura must realize that this could be her magical dream come true and go for it.

Question 10: Outcome?

Answer: **King of Swords (Reversed).** This reversed King is fickle and superficial. He is also a Gemini, like Laura. This indicates that the outcome is up to Laura and what she will decide.

Comment: With many cards reversed in this spread, it is apparent that Laura is not thinking clearly. She will have to make a decision, but she has time. This new relationship can work out if there is love between the two parties. Only they know the truth!

Marriage Spread for Glenda

CARDS IN THE SPREAD

1st	position	Knight of Pentacles
2nd	position	5 of Wands
3rd	position	Page of Wands
4th	position	Hanged Man (Reversed)
5th	position	4 of Wands (Reversed)
6th	position	Wheel of Fortune (Reversed)
7th	position	Hermit
8th	position	King of Swords
9th	position	4 of Cups
10th	position	Queen of Swords (Reversed)

READING

Question 1: Will I ever marry?

Answer: Knight of Pentacles. Glenda wants to marry if she finds a man of means who can support them both. She is waiting for an opportunity to go on vacation with him if he is willing to pay the bills.

Question 2: What kind of mate is compatible?

Answer: 5 of Wands. This card refers to a belief that one must fight to get ideas across at work and socially. With faith, one does not need to fight aggressively. Glenda wants a mate who will seek higher goals, use his will to gain recognition, and make money. Glenda's beliefs will bring her success if she is thinking positively.

Question 3: Will we have good methods of communication?

Answer: Page of Wands. This card shows an immature person who wants to work and have an active social life. Glenda and her friend rarely speak with each other. Her friend travels a good deal and stays busy.

Question 4: Will we both desire a commitment?

Answer: Hanged Man (Reversed). Glenda must be realistic and not just hang in there hoping things will change. She could meditate on this relationship to see if it is positive or futile. Perhaps she is committed but he is not.

Question 5: Will we have similar likes and dislikes?

Answer: 4 of Wands (Reversed). Glenda does not realize her thinking is out of balance. This card reversed shows no marriage, a lack of stability, and an unfruitful relationship. Glenda and her friend may have similar likes and dislikes but no basis for marriage.

Question 6: Will this person's family accept me?

Answer: Wheel of Fortune (Reversed). This is not the time for Glenda to gamble that his family will accept her. She must first make a relationship. Her friend is divorced and has two daughters, which could also present problems.

Question 7: How shall we find each other?

Answer: Hermit. Glenda has been divorced and has gained wisdom through her experiences in finding a mate. She must get in touch with her inner source and find the light to guide her to a loving partner.

Question 8: Will we be able to share our financial resources?

Answer: King of Swords. This is the card of a lawyer. Glenda may feel that she will need to protect herself legally or sign a prenuptial agreement in the event she does marry. This is a mental card and perhaps she should think about her beliefs.

Question 9: What can I do while I am waiting for my mate?

Answer: 4 of Cups. Glenda must realize that she is still holding on to her past love affairs (or her marriage). She needs to look at what is coming her way now—a new beginning in love—and grab it! Glenda must become balanced and not be ruled by her emotions. By changing her beliefs she will change her life.

Question 10: Outcome?

Answer: Queen of Swords (Reversed). Glenda does not want to stay single—she wants a marriage with equality and balance. She has problems and troubles of her own but Glenda would feel better about herself if she were married. She desires a mate—and soon!

Comment: Glenda must give up her past attitudes about men in order to have a positive relationship. She must not seek ineligible men and then hope to change them. If she feels this man is immature why desire the relationship to continue? Glenda is a Virgo and perhaps more critical and judgmental than she realizes, especially about men.

PREGNANCY SPREAD

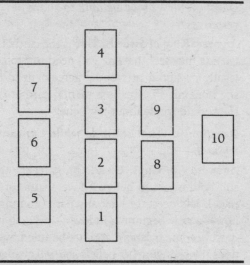

1. Am I ready for a child?
2. Do I have enough confidence to be a parent?
3. Will I be happy being a parent?
4. Will the other parent be supportive of the child?
5. Will I feel boxed in or lack of freedom because of the child?
6. What past behavior do I need to change to be better prepared for parenting?
7. Will I be able to give this child a good education?
8. Is there potential for the child to have health problems?
9. Will my parents be involved and supportive?
10. Final outcome?

Pregnancy Spread for Marcie

CARDS IN THE SPREAD

1st	position	8 of Pentacles (Reversed)
2nd	position	High Priestess (Reversed)
3rd.	position	8 of Wands (Reversed)
4th	position	3 of Pentacles (Reversed)
5th	position	Empress (Reversed)
6th	position	6 of Swords
7th	position	Queen of Cups (Reversed)
8th	position	10 of Cups
9th	position	Wheel of Fortune
10th	position	Fool (Reversed)

READING

Question 1: Am I ready for a child?

Answer: 8 of Pentacles (Reversed). Marcie lacks confidence in herself and feels she does not have the strength to have a child now. She also wants quick money but does not wish to work hard to get it. Marcie's new partner has money but there are conditions she may not be willing to accept.

Question 2: Do I have enough confidence to be a parent?

Answer: High Priestess (Reversed). Marcie does not know if she would make a good parent. She has some fixed ideas and tends to over-analyze her experiences. She is having an emotionally draining period trying to make decisions.

Question 3: Will I be happy being a parent?

Answer: 8 of Wands (Reversed). Marcie is lacking strength in her work and social activities. Her thoughts are unbalanced and could end her new relationship. Marcie is feeling vulnerable and insecure. She is definitely not committed to being a parent, so happiness is not the problem for her now.

Question 4: Will the other parent of the child be supportive?

Answer: 3 of Pentacles (Reversed). Marcie does not believe she creates her own money and has little faith or trust in her creative abilities, which would include a child. Her new love has money and the potential to inherit more, so he would be financially able to support a child.

Question 5: Will I feel boxed in or lack freedom because of a child?

Answer: Empress (Reversed). Marcie thinks she does not create her own experiences. She has problems with her mother and other women. She has a fear of losing her freedom and feels sexually unfulfilled, so she may not commit to a relationship now. The relationship may be over before it really starts. Without a relationship, she would not want a child.

Question 6: What past behavior do I need to change to be better prepared for parenting?

Answer: 6 of Swords (Reversed). Marcie has no choice about making changes—she must stay and face the issues and work them out. Marcie finds it difficult to make decisions, especially about having children. She is divorced and has no children.

Question 7: Will I be able to give this child a good education?

Answer: Queen of Cups (Reversed). Yes, if she marries this new love who has plenty of money and is a professional in his career. But Marcie is not being honest with this man—she is emotionally drained, resentful, and afraid to trust her heart.

Question 8: Is there a potential for the child to have health problems?

Answer: 10 of Cups. There could be a new cycle of change for Marcie. This card refers to love on a higher plane and, with the rainbow, some good luck. The scene is happy and healthy for the entire family. Marcie does not need to worry about the child's health.

Question 9: Will my parents be involved and supportive?

Answer: Wheel of Fortune. Marcie must take a chance on her life. Most parents welcome grandchildren and are supportive in many ways. Marcie must let go of old ties in her professional or personal life that have become a burden. It is time for new experiences and taking risks. The time is right for success!

Question 10: Final outcome?

Answer: The Fool (Reversed). Marcie is really not looking for new experiences of a lasting nature. She is lacking confidence, is sexually focused, and materialistic. Marcie needs to balance her pleasures, desires, and sexual attitudes realistically and have faith in the future.

Comment: Marcie is fearful of making another error in judgment. She has had a failed marriage and does not want to repeat that again. She confessed her need for freedom and to be able to get involved whenever she felt like it! Marcie's mother has not been a good example for stable marriages and Marcie is afraid she will repeat her pattern.

Pregnancy Spread for Betty

CARDS IN THE SPREAD

1st	position	The Sun (Reversed)
2nd	position	6 of Cups
3rd	position	Queen of Wands (Reversed)
4th	position	10 of Wands
5th	position	Knight of Cups (Reversed)
6th	position	Ace of Swords (Reversed)
7th	position	10 of Swords
8th	position	9 of Cups
9th	position	Death
10th	position	8 of Swords

READING

Question 1: Am I ready for a child?

Answer: The Sun (Reversed). Betty lacks courage and confidence at this time, which means she should not have a child now. Her low energy may be detrimental to herself and the child and lead to health problems in the future. Betty has been disappointed in her relationships and this may be one of the reasons she is not ready to commit to becoming a mother.

Question 2: Do I have enough confidence to be a parent?

Answer: 6 of Cups. Betty has made her own choices in love relationships. This card shows the potential to live in the past, or to bring someone from the past into her life again, and that may not be positive. Betty is divorced, but she does not want to be a single parent.

She is waiting for the right man to ask that important question, then she may consider having a child.

Question 3: Will I be happy being a parent?

Answer: Queen of Wands (Reversed). This Queen is a Leo, and people of this sign usually love children. They have great expectations and want their children to do well, as it is a reflection on the Leo ego. Betty is also career minded, so having a child may be a barrier to her ambitions.

Question 4: Will the other parent of the child be supportive?

Answer: 10 of Wands. According to this card the answer is "yes." Betty would not have to carry the burden alone and her job could get better along the way. The other parent will help Betty in many ways and also support the child.

Question 5: Will I feel boxed in or lack freedom because of the child?

Answer: Knight of Cups (Reversed). The lack of freedom is Betty's greatest fear. Just thinking about having a child has created an emotional drain and a strain on her relationship. Betty may be a procrastinator and not always honest. The Knight indicates that she did not get the message she was expecting and now she prefers not to make any decisions.

Question 6: What past behavior do I need to change to be better prepared for parenting?

Answer: Ace of Swords (Reversed). Betty must change some of her negative beliefs. Meditation and creative visualization can help her do this. She has little self-confidence or self-esteem, something that must be dealt with and resolved. All parents are apprehensive and want to do a good job raising their children. First-time parents feel a great deal of stress at this time, but experience is the only teacher when dealing with babies.

Question 7: Shall I be able to give this child a good education?

Answer: 10 of Swords. This card indicates big changes in store for Betty. Burdens will be lifted and her negative cycle is passing. There is plenty of time to be concerned with a complete education for a child who is not born yet.

Question 8: Is there a potential for the child to have health problems?

Answer: 9 of Cups. The wish card upright means you will get your wish. As she was thinking about health matters in regard to the child, I would say that the child would be in excellent health.

Question 9: Will my parents be involved and supportive?

Answer: Death. Betty's father is dead but her mother is alive and well and will be supportive, accepting the child under any circumstances. This child would show an end to a situation and a change for the better. This is the time for transformation, so let go of old experiences that have no meaning now in your life and grab new opportunities.

Question 10: Final outcome?

Answer: 8 of Swords. Betty has the strength to cope with all her experiences, and especially with her problems. She has a fear of making changes or taking risks. This can be a frustrating time for her, but only she can make the final decisions.

Comment: It is difficult to raise a child as a single parent, but many are attempting to do so. Betty is in her forties and will soon run out of options. Feeling she has made one "mistake" in marriage, she is reluctant to try again. These decisions are very personal and Betty is the only one capable of making them for herself. Her desires will win the day!

DIVORCE POTENTIAL

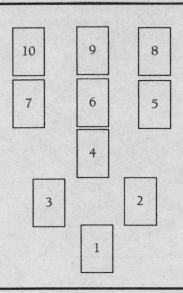

1. What reasons do I have for wanting a divorce?
2. Do I still love my mate?
3. Are we cheating each other or on each other?
4. Is money our problem? Do we use it as a tool against each other?
5. Are we still sexually compatible?
6. Why won't my mate accept more responsibility?
7. Does my mate have problems with liquor or drugs?
8. Do we try to control and abuse each other?
9. Can I change my negative feelings about my marriage?
10. Final outcome?

Chapter 6

ON THE MOVE

IN THIS CHAPTER, TRAVEL AND MAKING changes are highlighted. There are four spreads, three with sample readings and one without. The spreads are:

> Desire to Move
>
> Taking a Trip
>
> Relocation
>
> Planning a Trip

The last spread, "Planning a Trip," uses only six cards and should provide enough information in the reading to satisfy the querent. Each spread relates to changes of some kind for the individual and will allow them to make choices.

Once an idea has been planted in a person's mind, it must be thought over until a conclusion is reached. New ideas propel us forward and are always healthy. They take us out of our ruts and into a new realm of hope and curiosity. Looking forward to a new adventure can be very stimulating and the Tarot cards can give us these new ideas.

DESIRE TO MOVE

10	9	8
6		7
4		5
3	2	1

1. What are my concerns involving this move?
2. What is the conflict?
3. Will I be happy when I make this move?
4. How will my new home, new area, and work affect me?
5. What are my options about the move in the next few weeks?
6. What choices did I make in the past that are affecting me now?
7. Will I learn new skills at work or at home?
8. What does my financial future hold for me?
9. What are my hopes and fears about the move?
10. Final outcome?

Desire to Move for Andrea

CARDS IN THE SPREAD

1st	position	2 of Pentacles (Reversed)
2nd	position	4 of Pentacles
3rd	position	7 of Cups
4th	position	9 of Pentacles (Reversed)
5th	position	Lovers
6th	position	4 of Cups (Reversed)
7th	position	High Priestess
8th	position	Ace of Pentacles
9th	position	8 of Wands (Reversed)
10th	position	Page of Pentacles (Reversed)

READING

Question 1: What are my concerns involving this move?

Answer: 2 of Pentacles (Reversed). Andrea is a free spender and does not like to budget her money. She feels this makes her happy. Andrea fears the move will be expensive and she has only been in her new place about two years.

Question 2: What is the conflict?

Answer: 4 of Pentacles. Andrea, a senior citizen, does not know whether to rent or buy. Her conflict is trying to rent a nice place inexpensively. Andrea would like to hold on to her resources for security reasons. She also owns property that she has rented to others. Balanced energy is important now, due to her sudden desire to move.

Question 3: Will I be happy when I make this move?

Answer: 7 of Cups. This could be the path to happiness! Creative visualization can create an environment that makes all your dreams come true. If Andrea surrounds herself with positive thoughts, she will find the perfect place.

Question 4: How will my new home, new area, and work affect me?

Answer: 9 of Pentacles (Reversed). Andrea is not using wisdom in her finances. She has been a widow for several years and is still learning through experience about money matters. Andrea does not feel independent or able to do things on her own, but she is learning.

Question 5: What are my options about the move in the next few weeks?

Answer: Lovers. Andrea has the choice of staying where she is or moving back to her old stomping grounds. She is living close to her son, his wife, and Andrea's two grandchildren at this time. Her concern is for the two little ones, but she must decide soon.

Question 4: What choices did I make in the past that are affecting me now?

Answer: 4 of Cups (Reversed). Thinking about leaving her two grandchildren leaves Andrea emotionally drained. She admitted that her services were not being utilized by her daughter-in-law, and that was the reason she moved near the family. The decision Andrea made in the past was not a positive one for her.

Question 7: Will I learn new skills at work or home?

Answer: High Priestess. Andrea is smart and she

knows a lot that she could teach others. It will be a happier experience for Andrea to be among her old friends and making new ones.

Question 8: What does my financial future hold?

Answer: Ace of Pentacles. It appears that Andrea will have new beginnings with money providing some new financial aspect in her life that will be positive.

Question 9: What are my hopes and fears about the move?

Answer: 8 of Wands (Reversed). Andrea felt a lack of strength in dealing with her son's family. They did not meet socially and Andrea felt rebuffed at any other meetings with her daughter-in-law. Andrea fears she will not have much contact with this family if she moves. She hopes that all goes well with them and if she can help them, she will.

Question 10: Final outcome?

Answer: Page of Pentacles (Reversed). This card refers to the student who refuses to make money for schooling. The Page is an earth sign, practical and material. Andrea's two young grandchildren are both Taurus, and one will be entering school in September.

Comment: Regardless of what happens in her son's life, Andrea must still make decisions concerning her own. She can stay in touch with her grandchildren and do the best she can. This spread has shown a great deal of thinking about money, which is not healthy. Alice needs other interests to keep herself happy and involved with living her life to her fullest potential.

Desire to Move for Sylvia

CARDS IN THE SPREAD

1st	position	Justice (Reversed)
2nd	position	Hermit
3rd	position	Page of Pentacles
4th	position	7 of Cups (Reversed)
5th	position	2 of Cups (Reversed)
6th	position	9 of Wands (Reversed)
7th	position	Temperance
8th	position	Knight of Wands
9th	position	5 of Wands (Reversed)
10th	position	Wheel of Fortune

READING

Question 1: What are my concerns involving this move?

Answer: Justice (Reversed). There could be legal problems and Sylvia's health could be affected. She feels her landlord is very unfair and has had problems with other landlords; she dreads getting involved with a new one. Sylvia prefers owning her own home and has negative feelings about renting.

Question 2: What is the conflict?

Answer: Hermit. This card reflects an ending to some situation which has been handled in a positive manner. Sylvia must remember her past landlords and bless them—if she has negative feelings about them, the lesson is repeated. Using wisdom gained through experience brings success.

Question 3: Will I be happy when I make this move?

Answer: Page of Pentacles. This is the card of the student who is interested in making money, having a career, and reaching the top in their chosen field. Sylvia is ambitious, materialistic, and somewhat traditional. She sees greater opportunities for her career by making a move, as well as a chance to find happiness in a new area.

Question 4: How will my new home, new area, and work affect me?

Answer: 7 of Cups (Reversed). This card reversed does not assure success for Sylvia. There could be a loss through love or an emotional drain due to the move. Sylvia needs to do creative visualization and bring positive experiences into her life. She needs more faith and trust in her inner resources also.

Question 5: What are my options (about the move) in the next few weeks?

Answer: 2 of Cups (Reversed). Sylvia does not know she is in an emotionally stressful time. She is uncertain about her direction and there are no easy answers to her questions. Perhaps the move will take longer than she anticipated or her health will be affected by stress.

Question 6: What choices did I make in the past that are affecting me now?

Answer: 9 of Wands (Reversed). This card reversed refers to delayed plans and a lack of wisdom through experience. Sylvia was not open to new information in the past and may have been intolerant, critical, and judgmental. Some of the choices she made were not as positive as she thought.

Question 7: Will I learn new skills at work or at home?

Answer: Temperance. Sylvia has the potential to learn positive outlets for her energy, to have self-control, and achieve harmony with herself. She could also learn to have more patience and temper her ego needs. Sylvia will be able to learn new skills and perhaps get involved with a hobby or two.

Question 8: What does my financial future hold for me?

Answer: Knight of Wands. This messenger is bringing Sylvia information concerning work and social activities. There is good news relating to work, planning a trip, or a change of residence. The potential for a bright future and financial well-being seems to be the answer for Sylvia through this card.

Question 9: What are my hopes and fears about the move?

Answer: 5 of Wands (Reversed). Sylvia may fear some loss in her business if she moves. She does not desire to fight for her ideas and there is a lack of belief in her thinking. Sylvia's fears are focused on work and her social life. These fears may be keeping her from moving. Sylvia must use creative visualization about her business and believe that her inner source will guide her in the right direction.

Question 10: Final outcome?

Answer: Wheel of Fortune. This card indicates it is time to make changes, take a chance on a new venture, or travel. Gambling for fun or profit is also an option now. This would be a good time for Sylvia to make herself happy. The success that Sylvia is seeking is there for her—she needs a positive attitude and the desire to win!

Comment: There are many people involved with Sylvia, in her business and in her life (there are four Major Arcana cards and two Court cards, all telling of people affecting the querent). Sylvia is interested in change and her life has been full of it. Looking back at her experiences she sees that she has been successful in many areas of her life and that it need not change now. In the end, Sylvia is the one who must make the decision.

TAKING A TRIP

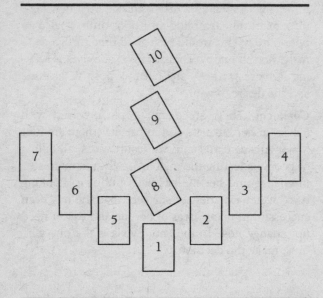

1. Where do I want to go?
2. Do I have enough money for a trip?
3. Should I go with friends or family?
4. Would I be happier on a tour?
5. Shall I go by plane?
6. Shall I go by boat or train?
7. What are the obstacles to my trip?
8. What kind of experiences will I have?
9. Will I meet someone special on this trip?
10. Outcome?

Taking a Trip for Tara

CARDS IN THE SPREAD

1st	position	Knight of Wands (Reversed)
2nd	position	High Priestess
3rd	position	Fool (Reversed)
4th	position	Page of Wands
5th	position	2 of Swords (Reversed)
6th	position	6 of Pentacles (Reversed)
7th	position	Queen of Swords
8th	position	9 of Swords (Reversed)
9th	position	5 of Cups (Reversed)
10th	position	4 of Swords (Reversed)

READING

Question 1: Where do I want to go?

Answer: Knight of Wands (Reversed). This Knight brings negative news regarding work and social activities, which brings delays and frustration at work and socially. She and several of her friends were planning a ship tour, but two of them have been fighting and refuse to go. They all want to back out, but Tara had her heart set on this trip. Tara is upset and angry over the turn of events.

Question 2: Do I have enough money for a trip?

Answer: High Priestess. Tara can afford this trip. She also has enough money to board her dog, whom she loves dearly and is not sure she wants to leave him.

Question 3: Should I go with friends or family?

Answer: Fool (Reversed). Tara needs more confidence and must take responsibility for making her own decisions. Tara's friends are acting immaturely and will miss out if they don't go. Tara has waited a long time for this trip and would be foolish to give it up.

Question 4: Would I be happier on a tour?

Answer: Page of Wands. This Page is eager to experience life and to be out in public. Tara needs change, new experiences, and excitement in her life as she rarely goes anywhere. She really wants to go on this cruise, which is a tour.

Question 5: Shall I go by plane?

Answer: 2 of Swords (Reversed). Tara does not want to fly. Although she's never flown before she has a fear of flying—a cruise is ideal for her. It is a leisurely way to travel with accommodations and food. Tara loves food, so all of her needs will be met! She does not want to face any problems, she just wants to go on her trip.

Question 6: Shall I go by boat or train?

Answer: 6 of Pentacles (Reversed). This vacation is already planned and a ship is the method of travel. Tara did agree to go and she can afford it—though she may fear losing her deposit. If her friends don't stop feuding, she may not go at all.

Question 7: What are the obstacles to my trip?

Answer: Queen of Swords. This card refers to a Libra woman—Tara is a Libra. Libras often have problems making decisions, fearing they are not right. This means that she creates her own obstacles and is hesitant to spend money on pleasure trips. Tara is used to being involved with problems and rarely takes time to be nice to herself.

Question 8: What kind of experiences will I have?

Answer: 9 of Swords (Reversed). Tara fears she will not enjoy herself on this trip. She is not in crisis, but she could create her own drama due to her insecurities, low self-esteem, or indecision (a Libra trait).

Question 9: Will I meet someone special on this trip?

Answer: 5 of Cups (Reversed). This card indicates that Tara refuses to believe in love or romance. She feels emotionally drained by her family and the loss of her parents. Tara is still playing old tapes about relationships and feels she has passed her prime. Tara is a loner, but still young enough to have a good relationship if she wants it.

Question 10: Outcome?

Answer: 4 of Swords (Reversed). Tara says she does not realize her problems and troubles. She is doing too much, she just got transferred on her job, and now this problem of "are we going or not." As of yet no decisions have been made and the trip is in limbo.

Comment: It has been a long time since Tara has done something nice for herself. After the reading she was almost convinced that she should go. One of her friends said she would go if Tara wanted to, and if only two take the trip, it will be fine. Of course, it is always more fun to have a group, but if that doesn't work, then go, even if you're alone. Why not? With all the reversed cards in this spread, chances are the trip will not be taken.

Taking a Trip for Jody

CARDS IN THE SPREAD

1st	position	Ace of Swords
2nd	position	The Lovers
3rd	position	The Moon
4th	position	4 of Wands
5th	position	Queen of Pentacles
6th	position	Devil (Reversed)
7th	position	3 of Swords
8th	position	10 of Cups
9th	position	The Hierophant
10th	position	Death

READING

Question 1: Where do I want to go?

Answer: Ace of Swords. Jody has been thinking about taking a vacation but is not sure where she would like to go. Jody feels there are new problems for her to resolve in her personal life and taking a trip would not be possible.

Question 2: Do I have enough money for a trip?

Answer: The Lovers. Jody must make decisions in her life. By accepting her responsibilities and having faith in her inner source she will realize her abundance. Now is the time for a trip or other happy events. This card is also a flag that Jody should take care of health needs now.

Question 3: Should I go with friends or family?

Answer: The Moon. Jody has all kinds of fears and

she must decide if she will be more comfortable among friends or family. Jody is swayed by her emotions and ends up feeling victimized. She does not always want to see the truth, and some of her friends are not loyal.

Question 4: Would I be happier on a tour?

Answer: 4 of Wands. This card relates to marriage, work, and social activities. Perhaps Jody would consider a tour where she could meet other people. She must realize it is her right to choose where to go and with whom. The affair will be balanced and fruitful, and that is good news!

Question 5: Shall I go by plane?

Answer: Queen of Pentacles. Jody will investigate the costs of the trip. She is an idealist and a perfectionist, so all the details will be worked out first. Jody works to make money and spending it is difficult for her. Her decision to go by plane will be predicated on cost.

Question 6: Shall I go by boat or train?

Answer: Devil (Reversed). Jody does have a preference. She wants to take a trip but she does not want to spend a lot of money. A boat trip would be Jody's choice, if the price is not exorbitant.

Question 7: What are the obstacles to my trip?

Answer: 3 of Swords. Jody must understand that she is creating her own problems. Her siblings want to take the trip too, but they can't agree on the time. Her decision must be based on her needs or she may miss her opportunity to go at all. Jody also feels that some members of her family are cheating her out of her vacation.

Question 8: What kind of experiences will I have?

Answer: 10 of Cups. Jody will have major changes in her love and emotional life. A trip is definitely slated for her at this time. There could be a new relationship, happiness, and harmony for Jody if she makes a positive decision for herself.

Question 9: Will I meet someone special on this trip?

Answer: The Hierophant. There is a potential that Jody will learn a great deal on this trip. It may be her inner source or someone she gets involved with. It will be a time to meditate, be silent, and trust her intuition.

Question 10: Outcome?

Answer: Death. Past situations are ending now and Jody has new ideas and plans for the future which indicate a change for the better. She must be open to love, let go of old habit patterns, and release resentments. She can use her energy to manifest a richer and fuller life.

Comment: Getting rid of old habit patterns is an important matter for everyone. Meditation and creative visualization will change a person's life. Jody must have faith in herself and her inner source to know she is never alone.

RELOCATION SPREAD

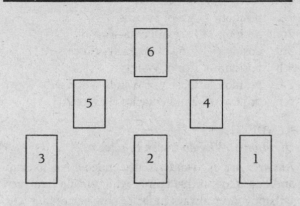

1. Why do I wish to relocate?
2. Is there a potential for a new job?
3. Is there a problem with my health in this area?
4. Will this move be successful financially?
5. Will I be happy in this new location?
6. Is it possible that this will be a permanent relocation?

Relocation Spread for Marty

CARDS IN THE SPREAD

1st position Ace of Swords
2nd position Page of Pentacles
3rd position King of Pentacles (Reversed)
4th position Ace of Wands
5th position Queen of Wands (Reversed)
6th position 2 of Pentacles (Reversed)

READING

Question 1: Why do I wish to relocate?

Answer: Ace of Swords. Marty ended a relationship and had a loss in his family which made him very unhappy. Aces always indicate new beginnings and Marty could see new problems arising for him.

Question 2: Is there a potential for a new job?

Answer: Page of Pentacles. The potential for a new job is great, as is further schooling to go along with the job. It could mean "on-the-job training," which Marty would accept.

Question 3: Is there a problem with my health in this area?

Answer: King of Pentacles (Reversed). There could be health problems for Marty if he becomes lazy, too focused on sensual pleasures, or impractical with money. Marty is a Virgo, and work and health issues are their main drives. Balance is the answer. Pentacles refer to Earth. These signs are Taurus (King of Pentacles), Virgo (Queen of Pentacles), and Capricorn (Page of Pentacles). Earth signs are material and practical when positive, but greedy and grasping when negative.

Question 4: Will this move be successful financially?

Answer: Ace of Wands. Marty will have new beginnings in his work and social life. There will be opportunities and potentials for him in this move both financially and socially. Marty should look forward to an exciting time during this period.

Question 5: Will I be happy in this new location?

Answer: Queen of Wands (Reversed). This card can indicate a domineering, demanding, and controlling boss. Marty will need to do good work, be punctual, and be efficient to please this person. If Marty pays attention to his job he can be happy.

Question 6: Is it possible that this will be a permanent relocation?

Answer: 2 of Pentacles (Reversed). Marty must learn as much as possible about his work, take care of his finances, and stay healthy. This card can indicate a lack of balance in money matters which Marty must overcome. It is possible!

Comment: This move could prove beneficial for Marty. It would change his environment and job and give him more potential options for new relationships. Now is the time to risk the move and make a new start.

PLANNING A VACATION

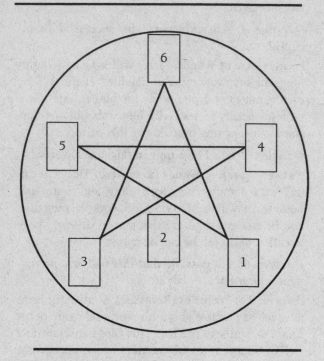

1. What kind of vacation do I prefer?
2. Shall I go alone?
3. Shall I go with others?
4. Will I enjoy myself and meet someone new?
5. Will there be any financial problems? Physical problems?
6. Do I need a vacation at this time?

Chapter 7

SEEKING SELF-KNOWLEDGE

THIS CHAPTER CONTAINS SPREADS THAT GIVE information about one's self. The spreads are:

> All About Me
>
> What Is My Destiny?
>
> Facing My Fears
>
> Old Habit Patterns
>
> Information Spread for the
> Past—Present—Future

The first four spreads have case studies that give you an idea about how to apply the Tarot cards to the spread. The last one, Information for the Past—Present—Future, does not have a case study, giving you the opportunity to try your intuition.

All five spreads are focused on an individual and one's experiences. Each digs deeply into the psyche and helps heal the person's negative feelings. If anyone is seeking help to change their life, these are the spreads that are the best for that purpose.

In doing the readings, the one most often chosen was All About Me.

ALL ABOUT ME

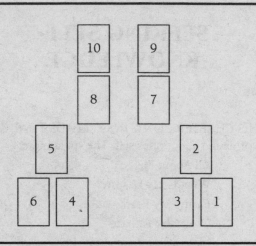

1. How do I get my ego needs fulfilled?
2. What influence does my mother still have on me?
3. Am I reacting to my father's influence?
4. Do I use my value judgment against myself?
5. Is my response to sex and my physical body positive?
6. Are my choices regarding relationships good for me?
7. Success is my goal. Do I have enough faith to succeed?
8. Are my financial affairs affected by my belief in lack?
9. Why do I feel victimized?
10. In what way can I change my life?

All About Me for Kerry

CARDS IN THE SPREAD

1st	position	8 of Pentacles
2nd	position	9 of Swords (Reversed)
3rd	position	The Empress
4th	position	10 of Swords (Reversed)
5th	position	10 of Cups
6th	position	Temperance (Reversed)
7th	position	3 of Cups
8th	position	2 of Cups
9th	position	Judgment (Reversed)
10th	position	5 of Swords

READING

Question 1: How do I get my ego needs fulfilled?

Answer: 8 of Pentacles. Kerry is a school teacher and has the strength to do a good job at work. Kerry is learning about politics and ego needs. She ran for the office of coordinator at her school, but lost by a narrow margin. Kerry was an apprentice at that time but is knowledgeable now. She must try another direction to fulfill her ego needs.

Question 2: What influence does my mother still have on me?

Answer: 9 of Swords (Reversed). Kerry lacked wisdom regarding her mother. She was in crisis regarding her problems but would not discuss them with her mother. There are ten children in Kerry's family and she wants her mom to love and accept her even though she is a rebel. The question is—what can her mom do to prove she loves Kerry?

Question 3: Am I reacting to my father's influence?

Answer: The Empress. Kerry's father is kind and gentle, and she loves him, but she may not have respected him. When dad is kind and gentle and mom (The Empress) rules the roost, a child is confused about who is the boss in the home. If Kerry needed protection as a youngster and her dad failed to be there, Kerry would feel vulnerable to males. This distortion occurs as dad is the male role model for all females in the home. Kerry's problems with men stem from this early conditioning and is changing some of her beliefs.

Question 4: Do I use my value judgment against myself?

Answer: 10 of Swords (Reversed). Kerry is still carrying her problems as a burden. She wants change, but the only way that can happen is if she changes her thinking. This card indicates that she may be judging herself too harshly.

Question 5: Is my response to sex and my physical body positive?

Answer: 10 of Cups. Yes, it is. Since Kerry has been working with Tarot her focus has changed and she has placed herself on a higher emotional level. The rainbow in the card is a sign of good luck and her home life has improved. The changes Kerry is making are healthy.

Question 6: Are my choices regarding relationships good for me?

Answer: Temperance (Reversed). Kerry's choices in relationships are not positive. There is a lack of balance in her or her partner. This has caused an emotional drain and much unhappiness for Kerry. She must realize that she has manifested her relationships and should reconsider her needs before she gets involved with a new partner.

Question 7: Success is my goal. Do I have enough faith to succeed?

Answer: 3 of Cups. This card verifies that Kerry makes her relationships, that she says, "I make my love and emotions, I make myself happy, and I make my pleasures." Her relationships do not seem to be positive and she shows a lack of faith in that portion of her life. Her ability to be successful in her job is without question.

Question 8: Are my financial affairs affected by my belief in lack?

Answer: 2 of Cups. Kerry knows that being in a good relationship is healthy, but she does not have a partner at this time. There seems to be a desire to help others and be loving, but not get too entangled herself. Perhaps she does not wish to spend money on a relationship just to have one. Kerry admitted that her finances are in sad shape and during the summer she intends to do extra work rather than spend her resources.

Question 9: Why do I feel victimized?

Answer: Judgment (Reversed). Kerry is not paying attention and lacks awareness in her affairs. She does not understand her own nature but is studying the Tarot now, which will give her insight into herself. She is beginning to realize what part she is playing in her own life and that she is victimizing herself.

Question 10: In what way can I change my life?

Answer: 5 of Swords. Kerry believes that relationships are too much trouble. She must not fight with others to get her own way all the time. She needs to feel confident and do what is right for herself. Changes will happen!

Comment: Kerry must release her pressures and enjoy life now. Let go of the battles and learn to love yourself!

All About Me for Gail

CARDS IN THE SPREAD

1st	position	3 of Wands (Reversed)
2nd	position	Devil
3rd	position	6 of Cups
4th	position	Ace of Pentacles (Reversed)
5th	position	Lovers (Reversed)
6th	position	4 of Cups
7th	position	7 of Swords (Reversed)
8th	position	6 of Pentacles (Reversed)
9th	position	Hermit
10th	position	6 of Swords (Reversed)

READING

Question 1: How do I get my ego needs fulfilled?

Answer: 3 of Wands (Reversed). Gail does not use creative visualization to get what she wants at work or socially. She does not make herself happy, go on trips, or communicate her desires. Gail must ask herself what her ego needs are in order to fulfill them.

Question 2: What influence does my mother still have on me?

Answer: The Devil. Gail feels oppressed by her mother. Her mother is focused on materialism and Gail is caught up in this influence. She can release herself any time by considering what she still wants from her mother.

Question 3: Am I reacting to my father's influence?

Answer: 6 of Cups. Gail's parents were divorced

when Gail was a little girl and she must make a choice—whether to hold on to past hurts and feelings of rejection or to forgive her dad. Gail is still waiting for love from her dad and it stands in the way of her relationships now.

Question 4: Do I use my value judgment against myself?

Answer: Ace of Pentacles (Reversed). Gail is judging herself and denying herself many life experiences. She just got a new job and makes more money but still feels insecure about her finances. Gail must ask herself how she values her life and whether she feels worthy. With these answers she may change her life.

Question 5: Is my response to sex and my physical body positive?

Answer: Lovers (Reversed). No. Gail may be refusing to seek a new partner because her last relationship is not completely over. She has no choice in the matter, except to finish it. Gail claims they are now friends.

Question 6: Are my choices regarding relationships good for me?

Answer: 4 of Cups. Gail is reflecting on her past relationships and not paying attention to what is being offered her. If past partners have not been positive, then she is not making good choices. By changing her beliefs, she also changes her choices. Gail must realize that she is out of balance and afraid to trust her heart for fear of being hurt. She, like the

Emperor, is the boss—independent, the initiator and full of good ideas. She is in charge of her life at all times.

Question 7: Success is my goal. Do I have enough faith to succeed?

Answer: 7 of Swords (Reversed). Gail is on the material and physical path. She does not have the faith in herself and often feels cheated. Gail also feels that other people are creating her problems rather than taking responsibility for her own actions. Success is always possible when a person has faith and trust in self.

Question 8: Are my financial affairs affected by my belief in lack?

Answer: 6 of Pentacles (Reversed). Gail feels she has no choice in financial matters and believes others are in control of her money. In fact, Gail may not want to share her resources and feels guilty. Sharing is natural, but a child forced to share may grow up resentful and refuse to be charitable. This attitude leads to belief in lack.

Question 9: Why do I feel victimized?

Answer: The Hermit. Gail feels unloved and alone. The Hermit is a Virgo card and her father is a Virgo. Dad is very critical and judgmental. Gail rarely sees him and she would like to have a better relationship with him. She is searching for a teacher or an inner guide.

Question 10: In what way can I change my life?

Answer: 6 of Swords (Reversed). Gail thinks she does not have a choice in changing her life, but she does. She must work her life out by changing her beliefs. Meditation and visualization are both methods that work. Thinking is destiny!

Comment: Parents are here to guide us, not carry us through life. Ask yourself what you want from them and then release them. Love and forgiveness—try it!

All About Me for Ruth

CARDS IN THE SPREAD

1st	position	10 of Swords
2nd	position	3 of Swords (Reversed)
3rd	position	Justice
4th	position	Knight of Pentacles (Reversed)
5th	position	6 of Cups
6th	position	Ace of Wands (Reversed)
7th	position	4 of Cups (Reversed)
8th	position	7 of Wands
9th	position	Emperor (Reversed)
10th	position	Devil (Reversed)

READING

Question 1: How do I get my ego needs fulfilled?

Answer: 10 of Swords. This card indicates that Ruth will have big changes in her problems and troubles. She feels pinned down and unable to move, but soon some of her burdens will be lifted. While these changes are taking place, her mental attitude will also change. If she is waiting for someone else to fulfill her ego needs, she will not be satisfied and perhaps disappointed. She must fulfill her own ego needs, not wait for others to do it.

Question 2: What influence does my mother still have on me?

Answer: 3 of Swords (Reversed). Ruth feels she does not make her own problems, that others are responsible for her trials. She has a rejection complex and feels insecure. Some of her friends are proving untrustworthy and she is confused. Ruth has always had problems with her mom and has never felt accepted by her. Ruth and her two daughters are now living with her mom and she feels some guilt about this. Ruth and a friend were planning to go on a cruise. Perhaps Ruth feels she should not go on this trip, spending her money on pleasure and enjoyment.

Question 3: Am I reacting to my father's influence?

Answer: Justice. Ruth admitted she felt abandoned by her dad. She is divorced and was upset to learn that her two daughters also felt abandoned by their father. As a child, Ruth loved her dad but felt rejected by him which set up a pattern for her in relationships with other men. Old habit patterns are difficult to break, especially when a person refuses to notice they keep repeating the same kind of experiences. Ruth agreed with this analysis.

Question 4: Do I use my value judgment against myself?

Answer: Knight of Pentacles (Reversed). This Knight does not bring good news about money or indicates that messages were not received. There are delays or failure of existing plans and Ruth may be denying herself sex, a home, or money due to her early experiences with her parents. She is using her value judgment against herself.

Question 5: Is my response to sex and my physical body positive?

Answer: 6 of Cups. Ruth is living in the past and her

memories are not very positive. She must take responsibility for her sexual exploits. She is overweight, which is not good for her body. If Ruth won't take care of her own needs, who will? She must make choices.

Question 6: Are my choices regarding relationships good for me?

Answer: Ace of Wands (Reversed). This card reflects no new beginnings in work or socially. Plans are canceled, there are delays and frustrations. Ruth does not respect males, so any relationship she attracts would be problematic. With understanding, she could change her attitude and change her life.

Question 7: Success is my goal. Do I have enough faith to succeed?

Answer: 4 of Cups (Reversed). Ruth does not realize she is keeping herself from success. She doesn't feel loved, fears a commitment, and has been disappointed in her relationships. She has unrealistic expectations, which stop her from getting involved. Ruth lacks balance, is not always honest, and admitted she was lazy. Faith to succeed comes from loving yourself and being willing to work toward your goals.

Question 8: Are my financial affairs affected by my belief in lack?

Answer: 7 of Wands. Ruth would like to feel she is doing superior work at her job. She has the ability to be successful in business or socially if she wants to be. She is a Cancer who needs to feel nurtured, safe, and secure. Having a home of her own is an important issue, yet she is living with her mother and working part-time.

Question 9: Why do I feel victimized?

Answer: Emperor (Reversed). Ruth does not realize her potential. She is fearful, immature, lacking balance, and not always honest. She could be a leader, boss, or in management. Ruth is not as warm and loving as she thinks and likes to control her environment. She is a good actress and believes the part she is playing. Ruth victimizes herself without realizing what she is doing. It is time to wake up and make changes.

Question 10: In what way can I change my life?

Answer: Devil (Reversed). Ruth must learn not to be so selfish, to feel secure, and not focus on material possessions. She could take more responsibility for her life and be an example for her daughters. Losing weight should be another priority and would make her proud of herself. If Ruth does these things she will change her life for the better!

Comment: What a person believes will manifest in their life. Consciousness is all we have to work with, and by paying attention to our thinking, we realize why our lives are the way they are. Ruth was able to see how she could change her life through the Tarot cards and their meaning as applied to the questions. If she takes a chance on herself, her life will become different and more enjoyable.

WHAT IS MY DESTINY?

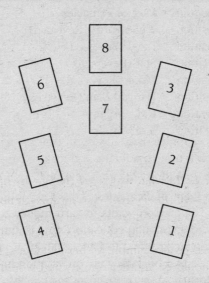

1. Will my life change soon?
2. Will a new relationship be exciting and sexy?
3. What chance is there for my ex-lover's return?
4. What is my potential to win or inherit money?
5. Is there a trip in my future?
6. Am I working out my karma?
7. Will I have a long and happy life?
8. Will I marry more than one time?

What Is My Destiny for Eric

CARDS IN THE SPREAD

1st	position	Page of Pentacles
2nd	position	7 of Swords (Reversed)
3rd	position	Devil (Reversed)
4th	position	Star (Reversed)
5th	position	Moon (Reversed)
6th	position	Hanged Man (Reversed)
7th	position	King of Cups
8th	position	4 of Wands

READING

Question 1: Will my life change soon?

Answer: Page of Pentacles. This Page indicates a scholar. This person wants to earn money to go to college and get a good education. Eric is almost fifteen and is determined to have a career in math or science. He and his family are on vacation in northern California, so there are changes in his life now.

Question 2: Will a new relationship be exciting and sexy?

Answer: 7 of Swords (Reversed). Eric does not have a relationship at this time. He did not like leaving his friends and almost refused to go with his family on this trip. Eric is too involved with his school work and a little immature to have a boy-girl relationship.

Question 3: What chance is there for my ex-lover's return?

Answer: Devil (Reversed). There is no ex- or present

lover for Eric. However, there is less selfishness or greed for material possessions. He is beginning to accept responsibility and face the reality of life. A change of diet will create better health.

Question 4: What is my potential to win or inherit money?

Answer: Star (Reversed). Eric is not optimistic about his career, life in general, or his goals. He has some vague ideas but gets bored easily. Eric must change his belief system now in order to have a more productive life. He is a Virgo, and people of this sign always feel they must "work" for anything they want. Winning would be against their belief!

Question 5: Is there a trip in my future?

Answer: Moon (Reversed). Eric is on that trip now. His mother is a teacher and plans family trips around educational destinations. This does not always please the rest of the family and they feel forced to go. Eric feels emotionally stressed not to have his way.

Question 6: Am I working out my karma?

Answer: Hanged Man (Reversed). This card refers to a person who does not trust their inner source, and does not accept new information easily. Eric is stubborn and physically and materially focused, which often puts him on the defensive. With maturity, some of these ideas will change and so will his life.

Question 7: Will I have a long and happy life?

Answer: King of Cups. This King represents an older man, so this would indicate a long life. When Eric grows up and becomes loving, caring, and nurturing, he will be happy. If Eric feels safe and secure in his professional life and within himself, he will have a good and joyous life.

Question 8: Will I marry more than one time?

Answer: 4 of Wands. Eric believes that when he gets married it will be permanent, balanced, and fruitful. He wants a solid relationship, for the two of them to work together, and to enjoy a good social life.

Comment: As can be seen, even at fourteen, a person's mind can be set with belief systems. Eric was apprehensive when I asked him to do this spread and all of the reversed cards indicate his unwillingness to participate. He is an intelligent youngster and works well with his hands. Eric has a lot of potential.

What Is My Destiny for Valery

CARDS IN THE SPREAD

1st	position	The World
2nd	position	7 of Swords (Reversed)
3rd	position	Page of Swords (Reversed)
4th	position	Wheel of Fortune
5th	position	4 of Swords (Reversed)
6th	position	5 of Wands
7th	position	Queen of Pentacles
8th	position	King of Cups

READING

Question 1: Will my life change soon?

Answer: The World. This card refers to success in all endeavors and the attainment of all goals. Valery must have faith that all is well. There will be new opportunities, trips, a new job, or a residential move. Valery is being supported by her inner source and victory is assured.

Question 2: Will a new relationship be exciting and sexy?

Answer: 7 of Swords (Reversed). If there is a new relationship, it will be over soon. Valery creates her own problems, though they are temporary. She may feel cheated or she could lose valuables and should take care when meeting new people. Valery must be prepared for new experiences by being open and honest.

Question 3: What chance is there for my ex-lover's return?

Answer: Page of Swords (Reversed). This Page has many troubles and is not a free thinker. Perhaps Valery's ex-lover is not a mentally stable person. She must examine her motives if she wants him to come back into her life.

Question 4: What is my potential to win or inherit money?

Answer: The Wheel of Fortune. This card indicates that it is time for Valery to take a chance, gamble, or take a trip. Now is the time to let go of old ties in business or relationships that are a burden. Valery must seek happiness, be positive, and stay healthy. Success in money matters is likely at this time.

Question 5: Is there a trip in my future?

Answer: 4 of Swords (Reversed). A trip for Valery at this time would be beneficial and rest could aid her health. She has been stretching the limits of her physical body and creating inner tension. She needs a change in her environment and a trip is the best answer.

Question 6: Am I working out my karma?

Answer: 5 of Wands. To work out her karma, Valery could try to be more loving and understanding of others. She has family strife and many challenges from co-workers. Valery wants to promote her own ideas at her work and social life, but ego needs can cause dissension in Valery's life and must be curbed.

Question 7: Will I have a long and happy life?

Answer: Queen of Pentacles. This Queen is involved with health matters and making money. She has critical views, is an idealist and perfectionistic. Valery is an Earth sign, and as a rule these people have strong and healthy bodies. She should have a long life and happiness will be her choice.

Question 8: Will I marry more than one time?

Answer: King of Cups. This King is emotional, loving, caring, and nurturing. When married, he is a good family man. As long as he feels secure in a situation, he will remain. Valery would do well to marry this type of man. If she does, one marriage is likely. If not, more than one marriage is probable.

Comment: Valery has a chance to change her life and be happy. She had three reversed cards in her spread, but overall the reading was positive. Her destiny looks very bright and shows a lot of potential. Valery should feel good about her future.

FACING MY FEARS

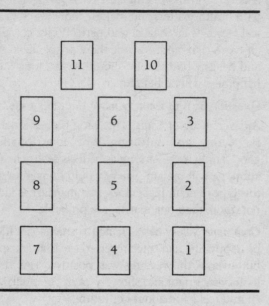

1. What am I afraid of?
2. Is my safety or security at risk?
3. Is there someone to whom I can communicate my fears to get help?
4. Are my fears focused at my workplace?
5. Do my fears concern sex or injury to my personal self?
6. Are these fears creating health problems for me?
7. Do my fears involve other people?
8. Do my fears stem from a lack of self-confidence or feelings of inadequacy?
9. Why do I feel like a victim?
10. What type of changes can I make to overcome my fears?
11. Final outcome?

Facing My Fears for Olivia

CARDS IN THE SPREAD

1st	position	10 of Pentacles (Reversed)
2nd	position	Page of Pentacles (Reversed)
3rd	position	Empress (Reversed)
4th	position	The Fool
5th	position	4 of Cups
6th	position	9 of Cups (Reversed)
7th	position	Ace of Wands
8th	position	Knight of Wands (Reversed)
9th	position	7 of Wands
10th	position	9 of Swords (Reversed)
11th	position	10 of Cups (Reversed)

READING

Question 1: What am I afraid of?

Answer: 10 of Pentacles (Reversed). Olivia fears not having money and does not feel that lack of finances can ever change for the better. Olivia is not prosperity minded, and it stems from her early childhood.

Question 2: Is my safety or security at risk?

Answer: Page of Pentacles (Reversed). Olivia did not continue her schooling and does not have a professional career. She feels that her earning power is limited and getting a good paying job is not possible. Olivia's security needs are in jeopardy and by going back to school her potentials can be increased. This will make her feel safe and secure in the future.

Question 3: Is there someone to whom I can communicate my fears and get help?

Answer: The Empress (Reversed). Olivia does not feel her mom will be of any assistance to her and has no relationship at this time, which leaves her feeling alone and vulnerable. Olivia needs a counselor and perhaps she can find one at school if she decides to go.

Question 4: Are my fears focused at my workplace?

Answer: The Fool. Olivia seems bored at her job. She wants new experiences, some activity and adventure in her life. Olivia must use caution because she does not have a relationship, is unhappy at home, and is not enjoying her life. She must pay attention to the environment and be confident that change will occur.

Question 5: Do my fears concern sex or injury to my personal self?

Answer: 4 of Cups. Olivia is hanging on to past experiences that were not positive. She may have been hurt emotionally and fears getting involved with the same type of experience. Olivia must change her mental attitude and trust her instincts.

Question 6: Are these fears creating health problems for me?

Answer: 9 of Cups (Reversed). This card indicates an emotional drain and unhappiness in love. Olivia suffered a loss through her relationship and by dwelling on this negativity, her health can be affected. She did not want to end this affair even though it was not positive. Olivia must learn to control her emotions and have a healthier outlook on life.

Question 7: Do my fears involve other people?

Answer: Ace of Wands. Olivia will be making new business and social contacts because she will have new beginnings and opportunities. If she fears these contacts, she will not be able to change her life.

Question 8: Do my fears stem from a lack of self-confidence or feelings of inadequacy?

Answer: Knight of Wands (Reversed). Olivia hates delays and frequently becomes frustrated both on the job and with her lack of social outings. She has not been very active socially, which makes her feel less self-confident.

Question 9: Why do I feel like a victim?

Answer: 7 of Wands. If Olivia feels superior on the job or socially, and she does not have a relationship, she may think others do not respect her. Olivia can have success and victory by treating her co-workers and personal relationships equally. Feeling like a victim is demeaning and Olivia must always respect herself.

Question 10: What type of changes can I make to overcome my fears?

Answer: 9 of Swords (Reversed). Olivia is in a crisis state that can soon come to a head. She must change her thinking and use wisdom in all situations. She must learn to trust her inner self and seek guidance from within. By recognizing her problems, answers will soon come to her—becoming aware is the first step toward a solution.

Question 11: Final outcome?

Answer: 10 of Cups (Reversed). Olivia's family makes her feel emotionally drained and she does not see immediate changes in her family affairs or relationships. Olivia must try to look on the positive side and do the best she can. She can only change herself but she wants to change others, which is impossible.

Comment: Olivia is going through a rough period in her life, but it will strengthen her resolve to make her life better. If she decides to go to school it could give her a new perspective. Her life is her choice and she must do the best she can.

OLD HABIT PATTERNS

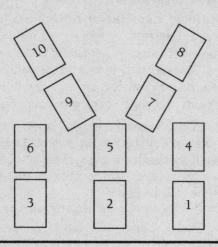

1. What are my past negative habit patterns?
2. How are they affecting my life?
3. What methods can I use to become aware of these patterns?
4. Are other people involved with my past patterns?
5. Will I be able to overcome these patterns?
6. What decisions must I make now?
7. Should I seek professional help?
8. Do I have the confidence to confront these old patterns?
9. What changes can I expect when I rid myself of these old habit patterns?
10. Final outcome?

Old Habit Patterns for Ellie

CARDS IN THE SPREAD

1st	position	King of Wands
2nd	position	The Tower
3rd	position	6 of Pentacles (Reversed)
4th	position	9 of Pentacles
5th	position	4 of Wands (Reversed)
6th	position	The Moon
7th	position	4 of Pentacles
8th	position	Hierophant (Reversed)
9th	position	Queen of Cups
10th	position	Wheel of Fortune (Reversed)

READING

Question 1: What are my past negative habit patterns?

Answer: King of Wands. Ellie has a good friend in business transactions and has some fears about trusting her own judgment. This King likes to start things but doesn't always stay to finish up, which Ellie enjoys doing. It should make her feel accomplished when she finishes any business deal in a·positive manner.

Question 2: How are they affecting my life?

Answer: The Tower. This card indicates Ellie must throw out her old habits and learn to depend on herself. This friend may decide to leave and Ellie must be prepared to have faith in her own judgment. She may have sudden insights into future events—if she is aware of this possibility she will not feel abandoned.

Question 3: What methods can I use to become aware of these patterns?

Answer: 6 of Pentacles (Reversed). This card indicates that Ellie does not make decisions regarding her finances. This is not wise of her and she must change her attitude about money immediately. Ellie must take control of her life and not lean on others. Meditation and seeking truth can make it easier for her to institute changes now.

Question 4: Are other people involved with my past patterns?

Answer: 9 of Pentacles. Ellie is in business and it is natural to assume that she has been involved with others. She enjoys being an independent woman of means and people are attracted to her because she is a winner. Although she has money, she seems to lack ideas that would increase her business, so she constantly seeks help from those who have creative skills.

Question 5: Will I be able to overcome these patterns?

Answer: 4 of Wands (Reversed). Ellie feels uncertain at this time. She fears her business may decline, that she will have a loss of finances, and that she will have no one to rely on. This is negative thinking, which can attract exactly those experiences she fears. Ellie can overcome these patterns by thinking positively, sending love to all, and having faith in herself.

Question 6: What decisions must I make now?

Answer: The Moon. Ellie must face the truth in all of her experiences and learn to control her negative thinking, fears, and doubts. Ellie would be wise to use her intuition to deal with her business. This card reflects attainment.

Question 7: Should I seek professional help?

Answer: 4 of Pentacles. Ellie needs a balanced attitude regarding money. If she feels she needs help, she should spend the money on herself. Ellie must look at truth and if it takes professional help, so be it!

Question 8: Do I have the confidence to confront these old patterns?

Answer: Hierophant (Reversed). At this time Ellie may not think she has the confidence, but this can change. She needs new information to help her grow and become a confident woman with faith in herself. Ellie has untapped inner resources and perhaps now is the time for her to become aware of her potential.

Question 9: What changes can I expect when I rid myself of these old habit patterns?

Answer: Queen of Cups. This Queen is powerful, intuitive, and intense. She desires control in her environment. Ellie can expect to be powerful, intense, and able to use her intuitive faculties. She can be in control of her life and make her own decisions. Then she can get in touch with her creative abilities.

Question 10: Final outcome?

Answer: Wheel of Fortune (Reversed). Ellie should not gamble or take risks at this time. No new ventures or serious relationships should be started now. Ellie needs to take care of her health and diet.

Comment: Ellie would be wise to seek professional help to become self-sufficient and in control of her life. She needs friends so she can enjoy herself away from work.

INFORMATION SPREAD
for the
PAST—PRESENT—FUTURE

Future	4	3	2	1
Present	4	3	2	1
Past	4	3	2	1

The Past: These cards can refer to yesterday or several years ago, but the information still has an influence on the querent's life.

The Present: These cards refer to the querent's thoughts and beliefs now.

The Future: These cards represent the querent's subconscious mind. Events may happen immediately or within the next few months.

TO BEGIN THIS SPREAD

Shuffle the cards and hand them to the querent. The querent should shuffle the cards and hand them back to you. They can cut the cards once, twice, or three times, whichever they prefer.

Place the first card face up on the first spot, beginning with the "Past" row, and then continue until all twelve cards have been laid out. Before you begin the reading, examine the spread. See which of the four elements are in the spread, check for repeat numbers (how many ones, twos, or threes, etc.) that appear in the spread. Also look at how many Major Arcana cards and Court cards are present. These indicate people involved with the querent. If there are many of these cards, this may indicate that there are too many people involved in the affairs of the querent. All of this information is helpful to you, the reader.

TO READ THIS SPREAD

When you speak of the past, remember to use such past tenses and phrases as "in the past." For cards relating to the present, your sentences should begin with "now." Future information could begin with "in the future this or that may happen."

This spread will show you how this person is thinking and through the spread you will have the opportunity to provide them new information that may change their thoughts or beliefs. This is a responsibility for the reader due to the nature of the information. The reader must have integrity and confidence. Above all, treat everything lightly and enjoy your abilities as a reader!

Chapter 8

SPIRITUAL SEEKERS

ALL FOUR SPREADS INCLUDED IN THIS CHAPTER
have case studies. Each spread refers to some aspect
of work being done by the individual to understand
their life and the necessity of birth.

The spreads are:

> Spiritual Aspiration
>
> Reincarnation
>
> Contacting Spirit Guides
>
> Soul Mates

Relax and give yourself plenty of time to work
with the fifteen questions included in the Reincarnation spread. The Soul Mate spread has eleven, while
Spiritual Aspiration has only seven. The Contacting
Spirit Guides has nine. These are all fun to do and
you will receive some valuable information at the
same time!

The different layouts are interesting to look at,
and be sure to involve the querent in conversation
during the readings. Try them out for yourself and
see what interpretations you arrive at.

SPIRITUAL ASPIRATION

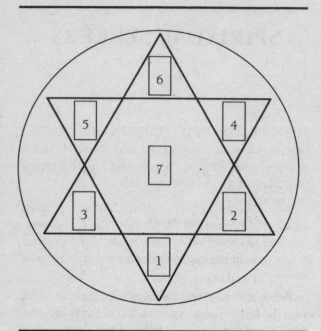

1. How do I work with my physical and material concerns?
2. How do I balance my desires?
3. Will I find a teacher soon?
4. What are the blocks to my enlightenment?
5. What changes must I make now?
6. Do I have choices to make?
7. Do I have enough faith in myself? Do I believe in a Higher Source?

Spiritual Aspiration for Jenny

CARDS IN THE SPREAD

1st	position	Emperor
2nd	position	10 of Wands
3rd	position	High Priestess
4th	position	8 of Swords (Reversed)
5th	position	7 of Pentacles
6th	position	Hermit (Reversed)
7th	position	6 of Wands

READING

Question 1: How do I work with my physical and material concerns?

Answer: Emperor. Jenny realizes she is the boss, leader, and initiator of her actions. She is independent and has good ideas. Jenny works with her inner source to help her control her physical and material desires.

Question 2: How do I balance my desires?

Answer: 10 of Wands. Jenny balances her desires by refusing to accept the burdens of others. There are constant changes in Jenny's workplace and new people to deal with every day and she could have a lot of stress if she did not maintain this balance.

Question 3: Will I find a teacher soon?

Answer: High Priestess. This card infers that Jenny knows a great deal. She must listen to her inner source for guidance and then apply the knowledge. She must find her teacher within.

Question 4: What are the blocks to my enlightenment?

Answer: 8 of Swords (Reversed). Jenny does not feel she has the strength to overcome her problems and thinks she is in bondage. However, it is only a belief and can be changed at any time through meditation. The real problem could be fear of enlightenment and the ensuing responsibilities.

Question 5: What changes must I make now?

Answer: 7 of Pentacles. The mental path Jenny must take now is how to harvest the money she gets. She must not let her ego get in the way of her desire to be of service. Jenny might get in touch with her inner source and be guided to her wish.

Question 6: Do I have choices to make?

Answer: The Hermit (Reversed). Jenny has a lack of wisdom through her experiences. There could be fear or some insecurity that must be dealt with first. Jenny has choices to make, but they must be made with confidence and an open mind. She may not be in touch with her inner teacher at this time.

Question 7: Do I have enough faith in myself? Do I believe in a Higher Source?

Answer: 6 of Wands. This is a card of victory! Jenny can be victorious by making right choices at work and socially. She must balance her desires and ego needs with faith in herself and her inner resources.

Comment: Jenny would like to start a spiritual center to teach spiritual values. It could happen!

Spiritual Aspiration for Lilly

CARDS IN THE SPREAD

1st	position	2 of Pentacles (Reversed)
2nd	position	Knight of Swords
3rd	position	Wheel of Fortune
4th	position	Ace of Wands
5th	position	9 of Swords (Reversed)
6th	position	2 of Swords (Reversed)
7th	position	4 of Wands

READING

Question 1: How do I work with my physical and material concerns?

Answer: 2 of Pentacles (Reversed). Lilly feels she does not know how to handle money. She does not like to budget and she is materialistically focused. She likes to spend money on others as well as herself, so she is not greedy.

Question 2: How do I balance my desires?

Answer: Knight of Swords. Desires are overcome through realization. Lilly is a Leo and a very strong individual. She likes to help others who are not as strong or able as she. Lilly attracts people who have problems and then becomes embroiled in them herself. She has her own problems that she must attend to first. If Lilly would balance herself then she could be an example for others to follow.

Question 3: Will I find a teacher soon?

Answer: Wheel of Fortune. Now is the time for Lilly to make changes, to take a trip or a gamble. Let go of old ties—business or personal—that are a burden. Seek happiness during this peak period. Lilly should realize that life is experience and everything she does or has done makes her who she is today. Life has been her teacher and with the changes she makes she may find a teacher she could accept.

Question 4: What are the blocks to my enlightenment?

Answer: Ace of Wands. Lilly desires new beginnings in her work and social life. She wants excitement, pleasure, and relationships. Enlightenment comes through meditation, doing good works, and the inward search for one's source. When Lilly ends her focus on just the "outer" world she will begin her enlightenment.

Question 5: What changes must I make now?

Answer: 9 of Swords (Reversed). The changes Lilly must make include overcoming problems, trusting her intuition, and evaluating her experiences to gain wisdom. She must have faith in herself, meditate, and stop having great expectations that lead to disappointments. Leo is the sign of the ego, which must be controlled in spiritual work.

Question 6: Do I have choices to make?

Answer: 2 of Swords (Reversed). Since Lilly does not want to know or see her problems and troubles, she will continue to have them. She has a fear of seeing herself in a true light, which could give her freedom. Her illusory thinking about life and the world in which she lives gives her a materialistic focus, and she must choose between this and spiritual desires.

Question 7: Do I have enough faith in myself? Do I believe in a Higher Source?

Answer: 4 of Wands. Lilly realizes that her work and social activities are fruitful. She may desire marriage at this time rather than the pursuit of spiritual aspirations. She does not have as much faith in herself in relationships as she does in her work abilities. There is a possibility that she does believe in a Higher Source. But what she wants now is to buy a condominium!

Comment: Lilly is a stewardess and enjoys her work. She likes the excitement of going to foreign countries and meeting people. She is divorced but may want to get married again. She is not motivated to turn her full attention to spiritual work in the present.

REINCARNATION SPREAD

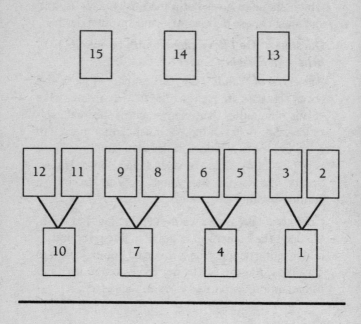

1. Who was I in my last life?
2. Was I married?
3. Was I happy in this past life?
4. What kind of work did I do in that life?
5. Was I an honorable person?
6. What type of problems and challenges did I deal with?
7. Was I a famous person?
8. Was my health good during my past life?
9. How did I die?
10. Did I have a soul mate?
11. Is my present love relationship someone I knew during my past life?
12. Am I linked to my parents of today from my past life?
13. Are any other members of my family from a past life of mine?
14. What do I need to learn during this lifetime?
15. Will I reincarnate after this life?

Reincarnation Spread for Daniel

CARDS IN THE SPREAD

1st	position	7 of Swords (Reversed)
2nd	position	5 of Wands (Reversed)
3rd	position	Hermit (Reversed)
4th	position	2 of Cups
5th	position	Fool
6th	position	Strength
7th	position	Empress
8th	position	4 of Pentacles (Reversed)
9th	position	Page of Swords
10th	position	2 of Pentacles
11th	position	8 of Wands (Reversed)
12th	position	6 of Wands
13th	position	9 of Pentacles (Reversed)
14th	position	9 of Cups
15th	position	9 of Wands (Reversed)

READING

Question 1: Who was I in my last life?

Answer: 7 of Swords (Reversed). Daniel was not happy in his last life. He was jealous, materially focused, and in relationships that were not positive. According to the cards in his spread, he had problems with work and money situations. Daniel may have been a woman (indicated by the presence of The Empress found in the 7th position of this spread).

Question 2: Was I married?

Answer: 5 of Wands (Reversed). This card shows the possibility that Daniel was married and they did not have a good relationship and he may not have fought for his rights. Daniel needed more faith and confidence in himself.

Question 3: Was I happy in this past life?

Answer: Hermit (Reversed). Daniel lacked wisdom or insight, was selfish and intolerant. He was focused on physical and material possessions. If he'd been happy, he would not have been greedy in his need for these things.

Question 4: What kind of work did I do in that life?

Answer: 2 of Cups. This card may indicate that Daniel sought marriage as a means to fulfill his life. If he was a female, that would have been the natural thing to do. Being a wife, mother, and nurturer would be the job during that period.

Question 5: Was I an honorable person?

Answer: Fool. This card would show that Daniel (in that life) was interested in new experiences, activity, and adventure and did not use his intelligence wisely. He may have been honorable, but others may have judged him harshly.

Question 6: What type of problems and challenges did I deal with?

Answer. Strength. Daniel had problems with leadership, controlling his passions, and resisting temptation. All of these things were challenges to his place in life. Daniel was also artistic and creative during that lifetime.

Question 7: Was I a famous person?

Answer: The Empress. This card would suggest that Daniel was a famous person, perhaps a female, and a powerful figure in that environment. Fame may have been Daniel's, but he was also creative, a communicator, and loving and nurturing.

Question 8: Was my health good during my past life?

Answer: 4 of Pentacles (Reversed). There may have been a lack of balance in Daniel's life and he may have been too busy enjoying himself. Excessive gambling and spending or money problems would have affected his health adversely.

Question 9: How did I die?

Answer: Page of Swords. This card indicates that Daniel might have died young by the sword or guillotine. He had many desires, was naive, unconventional, and extroverted. Daniel did not pay attention to his life and circumstances, and that may have cost him his life.

Question 10: Did I have a soul mate?

Answer: 2 of Pentacles. It appears that Daniel had a soul mate that tried to maintain a balance in money and health. If Daniel wanted material possessions, to live life to the fullest, or wanted new adventures constantly, the ability to juggle everything fell to the soul mate. The 2 of Cups and 2 of Pentacles in the spread could indicate a mate or close relationship.

Question 11: Is my present love relationship some-one I knew during my past life?

Answer: 8 of Wands (Reversed). Daniel claims he does not have a love relationship at this time. He has had several involvements during this life but none that lasted. Perhaps he sensed some connection with past loves and fears repeating his experiences from his past life.

Question 12: Am I linked to my parents of today from my past life?

Answer: 6 of Wands. This card refers to making choices, being responsible and taking control of one's life. It states that Daniel made a choice about his parents in this life adventure. He can be victorious in his chosen work and social life.

Question 13: Are any other members of my family from a past life of mine?

Answer: 9 of Pentacles (Reversed). This card infers that some family members were connected through finances. Daniel is having to learn to work and take care of his own financial burdens. He cannot depend entirely on family, relationships, or others for support.

Question 14: What do I need to learn during this lifetime?

Answer: 9 of Cups. Daniel must use wisdom in his experiences. He will get his wish concerning his love and emotional needs. This is the "wish" card and when it appears upright, it means you will get your wish. Daniel must learn to love wisely, have self-confidence and self-esteem.

Question 15: Will I reincarnate after this life?

Answer: 9 of Wands (Reversed). Daniel feels that he would rather not. He does not like competition in the business world or in society, for he is more passive and would prefer to handle his affairs in a more spiritual way. With four of the number 9 cards present in this spread (including The Hermit) this may be his last trip into life.

Comment: It is all conjecture supported by very little proof, but there is information in our cells regarding past, present, and future. There are many reversed cards in Daniel's spread. It seems that he does not have a good memory regarding his past life. Work and money were issues for Daniel and it seems the same ones are happening to him again. What is the lesson, Daniel?

Reincarnation Spread for Renee

CARDS IN THE SPREAD

1st	position	6 of Cups (Reversed)
2nd	position	4 of Cups (Reversed)
3rd	position	The Tower
4th	position	5 of Cups (Reversed)
5th	position	The Empress
6th	position	Death
7th	position	Knight of Cups
8th	position	Strength
9th	position	King of Wands
10th	position	10 of Swords
11th	position	Queen of Wands
12th	position	3 of Wands
13th	position	6 of Wands
14th	position	Wheel of Fortune
15th	position	9 of Swords

READING

Question 1: Who was I in my last life?

Answer: 6 of Cups (Reversed). Renee was a person who did not make her own choices. She was emotionally drained and there was a potential for illness in her past life that may have afflicted her severely. She may have never married. Perhaps irresponsible, she may have refused to make decisions and stayed close to her family.

Question 2: Was I married?

Answer: 4 of Cups (Reversed). Renee may have been afraid of an emotional relationship. She feared being hurt by someone she loved, so she may not have married. There may have been a lack of balance, a missing father figure, or some dishonesty.

Question 3: Was I happy in this past life?

Answer: The Tower. This card indicates that Renee received some enlightenment during this past life. She had some positive experiences and learned a great deal. She managed to get rid of some false ideas and old habit patterns. There was strife, but there were also some good times.

Question 4: What kind of work did I do in that life?

Answer: 5 of Cups (Reversed). This card declares that Renee did not believe in love. There may have been several losses in the family, relationships, or friends that hurt her. She felt she might have been a church leader. There may have been great disappointment for her during that time and the church offered some protection.

Question 5: Was I an honorable person?

Answer: The Empress. Yes. Renee was a creative lady. She knew how to communicate with others, loved to have good times, and enjoyed traveling. Renee cared about others, was nurturing, and sharing.

Question 6: What type of problems and challenges did I deal with?

Answer: Death. There were lessons for Renee regarding death and dying. She may have gotten in the way of other people's karma by trying to save them.

Transformation was a challenge for Renee and people were constantly going in and out of her life.

Question 7: Was I a famous person?

Answer: Knight of Cups. Renee was well known as she was forever receiving messages of all kinds. She was a person who wished to do service work and to help others. Renee may have traveled and visited far-off places. She was always getting invitations to attend functions from family, friends, and others in high standing.

Question 8: Was my health good during my past life?

Answer: Strength. Yes, it was. Renee was able to handle her desires and maintain a balance in that life. She had courage, fortitude, and used her power wisely.

Question 9: How did I die?

Answer: King of Wands. Renee felt that she died alone. This is an Aries card and could show some type of mental problems or a stroke. As Aries rules the head, she may have been shot in the head by a man as she thought. Whatever happened, it was a sudden death.

Question 10: Did I have a soul mate?

Answer: 10 of Swords. During that life, Renee experienced major changes in her problems and sought to raise her consciousness. She was very busy trying to lift her burdens and overcome negative experiences and did not feel her soul mate made an appearance during that lifetime.

Question 11: *Is my present love relationship someone I knew during my past life?*

Answer: Queen of Wands. Renee indicated she had no love relationship at this time. This is a Leo card—perhaps she is trying to find a partner who is a Leo?

Question 12: *Am I linked to my parents of today from my past life?*

Answer: 3 of Wands. Renee feels a strong link to her mother. She also feels she was involved with her father, but not as closely.

Question 13: *Are any other members of my family from my past life?*

Answer: 6 of Wands. Renee has nine siblings and feels that some of them were involved in her past life. She thinks that some were very good workers and successful during that time.

Question 14: *What do I need to learn during this lifetime?*

Answer: Wheel of Fortune (Reversed). This card reversed signifies that Renee did not have major lessons to learn in that lifetime. It was not the time to begin new ventures or take chances and she needed to be honest in all her experiences. The lessons now relate to more stability and less risk taking with her life and time.

Question 15: Will I reincarnate after this life?

Answer: 9 of Swords. This card indicates wisdom gained through experience with problems and troubles. The thought put Renee in crisis as she felt this time was sufficient. Renee said, "Do this again? Never!"

Comment: The Empress card may indicate that Renee held a high position in this past life. It seems she had some unfortunate experiences, but her life was devoted to service and she did her best.

CONTACTING SPIRIT GUIDES

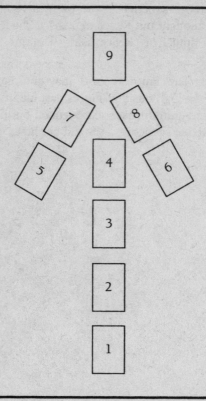

1. Are there spirit guides for everyone?
2. How can I contact my spirit guides?
3. Will I make contact with my spirit guides soon?
4. Will we communicate mentally only?
5. Have my spirit guides been with me always?
6. Will my guides give me information about my work, home matters, and relationships?
7. Can my guides teach me about other realities?
8. Do spirit guides appear in physical form?
9. Final outcome?

Contacting Spirit Guides for Shirley

CARDS IN THE SPREAD

1st   position   6 of Wands
2nd   position   7 of Pentacles (Reversed)
3rd   position   The Hermit (Reversed)
4th   position   2 of Swords
5th   position   King of Wands (Reversed)
6th   position   The Fool (Reversed)
7th   position   10 of Wands (Reversed)
8th   position   The World
9th   position   Knight of Swords (Reversed)

READING

Question 1: Are there spirit guides for everyone?

Answer: 6 of Wands. The answer is yes for everyone who believes in spirit guides. Making decisions and winning is what this card is saying. Shirley is using her will and energy in positive ways mentally, physically, and emotionally. Perhaps she will contact her guides soon.

Question 2: How can I contact my spirit guides?

Answer: 7 of Pentacles (Reversed). It is possible that Shirley does not have enough faith in herself and she may be lacking confidence. Shirley is being positive in many ways, but her belief in spirit guides may not be included. Through meditation and concentration Shirley could contact her guides—it is a good way to get started.

Question 3: Will I make contact with my spirit guides soon?

Answer: The Hermit (Reversed). Shirley lacks wisdom through her experiences, can be closed minded and prejudiced. She must examine her fears in the event she contacts her guides as it could create problems for her mentally. Shirley must realize her guides are there to help, not injure her.

Question 4: Will we communicate mentally only?

Answer: 2 of Swords. Shirley says she knows about her spirit guides but she doesn't want to "see" them. She is not using her intuition, so things are not clear. If Shirley does not want to see her guides, when she does make contact, it can only be mentally.

Question 5: Have my spirit guides been with me always?

Answer: King of Wands (Reversed). The possibility is that your guides do not stay in one place all the time. This card is an Aries, and these people like to be on the go. It may be that Shirley has guides who like to play and have fun (Aries types can be like children). This could be a message for Shirley to lighten up.

Question 6: Will my guides give me information about my work, home matters, and relationships?

Answer: The Fool (Reversed). Shirley must take responsibility and balance pleasure, sexual needs, and the other desires in her life. Her guides will try to focus her attention on spiritual matters and let her make decisions about worldly issues.

Question 7: Can my guides teach me about other realities?

Answer: 10 of Wands (Reversed). Shirley must realize that her guides can teach her many things. She is seeking release from burdens in her professional and social lives but does not seem to be interested in spiritual information. Shirley feels this is a "fad" that will soon pass—but she is not right. Spirit is and will always be. The guides are with us if we acknowledge them.

Question 8: Do spirit guides appear in physical form?

Answer: The World. This card is called "Cosmic Consciousness." There is nothing that spirit guides cannot do. When miracles happen, the guides are involved. Usually, the guides are seen in consciousness, but who knows the truth? Shirley must have faith and trust.

Question 9: Final outcome?

Answer: Knight of Swords (Reversed). Shirley may not get any messages at this time regarding her spirit guides, but she should keep trying if she is sincere.

Comment: There are many new students in spiritual work and Shirley is one of them. Many are in a hurry to attain the knowledge others have spent years gathering. In time we shall all make the grade. Shirley will make it sooner or later.

Contacting Spirit Guides for Penny

CARDS IN THE SPREAD

1st	position	5 of Swords
2nd	position	Temperance
3rd	position	The Chariot
4th	position	7 of Wands (Reversed)
5th	position	6 of Swords
6th	position	7 of Cups
7th	position	6 of Cups
8th	position	Hanged Man (Reversed)
9th	position	4 of Cups

READING

Question 1: Are there spirit guides for everyone?

Answer: 5 of Swords. This card suggests that Penny does not believe in spirit guides. She desires to overcome others due to her own ego needs and this can lead to rash behavior on her part. Her mental attitude is not positive, and may bring empty victory.

Question 2: How can I contact my spirit guides?

Answer: Temperance. Penny must trust her inner source for guidance and have faith that she will be able to contact her own special guides—meditation is a very good way to do this. Patience is another virtue that Penny must cultivate as she balances her desires with wisdom.

Question 3: Will I make contact with my spirit guides soon?

Answer: The Chariot. This card indicates that now is

the time to use one's mental powers to control destiny and be victorious. The Charioteer represents Penny's Higher Self and she must trust Him to guide her in all of her affairs. She must have faith that the source is within her and she will soon make contact.

Question 4: Will we communicate mentally only?

Answer: 7 of Wands (Reversed). Penny is too focused on her physical and material needs at this time. Her path is unclear and there is uncertainty about her future. There must be more faith and trust in the Higher Self in order to make any kind of contact—mentally or spiritually.

Question 5: Have my spirit guides been with me always?

Answer: 6 of Swords. Penny has a lack of knowledge or realization about her spirit guides. She is too focused on her problems and troubles and needs more faith in herself. Her Higher Self is always with her (as with all of us). Penny must acknowledge this Presence within her to realize It or They are there. Penny has a choice: run away from her problems and troubles or stay and see them through, knowing the Higher Self is helping her.

Question 6: Will my guides give me information about my work, home, and relationships?

Answer: 7 of Cups. This card indicates that through creative meditation it will lead her to correct responses. Her spirit guides are there to help her through all her experiences.

Question 7: Can my guides teach me about other realities?

Answer: 6 of Cups. Penny must make the choices about what she wants to know. She must be careful not to live in the past or focus her energies on past relationships. Penny has a world of knowledge within herself and her guides can give her this information if she has the ability to accept it.

Question 8: Do spirit guides appear in physical form?

Answer: Hanged Man (Reversed). Penny is easily fooled by others and she should be aware of living in fantasy or illusion. She does not have faith or trust in a Higher Self and wants visual proof of Its existence. This may not happen, but it does not mean the Higher Self does not exist.

Question 9: Final outcome?

Answer 4 of Cups. Penny realizes she lives in the past in her relationships. She must overcome depression and become aware that new opportunities await her. Old habit patterns must be discarded by her realization that she is the one in charge of her life, love, and emotional well-being.

Comment: Just as we take other things for granted we must be prepared to accept our inner guidance. Penny needs faith and trust in this concept. As it is said, "when the student is ready, the teacher appears."

SOUL MATE SPREAD

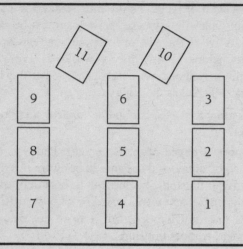

1. How do I contact my soul mate?
2. Is my soul mate in the physical world now?
3. Is it possible to communicate with my soul mate now?
4. What can I do to bring my soul mate into my life?
5. Is my soul mate a free spirit?
6. Have we been in relationships in the past?
7. Do I need to study or learn anything about soul mates?
8. Will there be harmony and well-being between us?
9. How can I learn to love and accept my soul mate?
10. What changes can I make while I wait for my soul mate?
11. Final outcome?

Soul Mate Spread for Meredith

CARDS IN THE SPREAD

1st	position	Justice
2nd	position	3 of Pentacles
3rd	position	Queen of Wands (Reversed)
4th	position	4 of Pentacles (Reversed)
5th	position	3 of Cups
6th	position	The Sun (Reversed)
7th	position	3 of Swords
8th	position	4 of Cups (Reversed)
9th	position	10 of Wands (Reversed)
10th	position	King of Pentacles (Reversed)
11th	position	8 of Wands

READING

Question 1: How do I contact my soul mate?

Answer: Justice. Meredith can contact her soul mate through acts of kindness, caring, and nurturing others. She must use discrimination in her experiences and treat others as she would like to be treated. Meditation and creative visualization are good ways to do this. Meredith must have faith in her inner source and then she will succeed in contacting her soul mate.

Question 2: Is my soul mate in the physical world now?

Answer: 3 of Pentacles. This card refers to the physical world (pentacles)—indicating the possibility of Meredith's soul mate being in the world at this time. The 3 of Pentacles speaks of a master craftsman—artistic and good at what they do. They have faith in their abilities and making money through their work. Meredith needs to get busy with her visualization now!

Question 3: Is it possible to communicate with my soul mate now?

Answer: Queen of Wands (Reversed). This card reversed depicts a Leo man. Anytime Meredith is ready, she can begin to contact her soul mate. Through meditation and creative visualization Meredith will be able to make this contact in a matter of weeks if she is persistent!

Question 4: What can I do to bring my soul mate into my life?

Answer: 4 of Pentacles (Reversed). Meredith must put herself in a balanced state. She may be a spendthrift, a gambler with a need to understand the value of money. Meredith may be involved with negative experiences that she must change, or possibly find herself dealing with health issues. Her beliefs need to be altered and her thinking directed into positive channels.

Question 5: Is my soul mate a free spirit?

Answer: 3 of Cups. The answer is yes. This soul mate is happy, has good times, and desires to travel. The soul mate is creative through the arts, music, and literature. Meredith could learn a great deal from her soul mate about enjoyment in life.

Question 6: Have we been in relationships in the past?

Answer: The Sun (Reversed). The Sun card is Leo, a sign also seen in question 3. If there was a past encounter it was not positive. Reversed, this card speaks of dishonesty, a lack of courage, and low self-esteem. Whether this information relates to Meredith or her soul mate, it does not show a great relationship. Meredith probably was not in a relationship with her soul mate in the past.

Question 7: Do I need to study or learn anything about soul mates?

Answer: 3 of Swords. Meredith may study and learn about anything that interests her. If her friends are into soul mates and she is jealous of them, she can follow the crowd. Meredith should know, however, that she makes her own problems and doing spiritual work can create more problems for her than she realizes. It would be healthier to know something about "higher knowledge."

Question 8: Will there be harmony and well-being between us?

Answer: 4 of Cups (Reversed). Meredith feels she will be disappointed in this relationship with her soul mate. She is inexperienced in relationships and does not have much faith or trust in them. There can be harmony and well-being if Meredith will relax and be confident that her soul mate cares about her.

Question 9: How can I learn to love and accept my soul mate?

Answer: 10 of Wands (Reversed). Meredith must make changes in her life. She feels stagnant both at work and in her social life and is looking for alternatives. If her life is dull, does she expect her soul mate to make her world thrilling? Meredith must evaluate her expectations and decide whether she is ready to accept her soul mate honestly.

Question 10: What changes can I make while I wait for my soul mate?

Answer: King of Pentacles (Reversed). Meredith must overcome some negative traits within herself such as selfishness and being lazy and impractical. She could learn to be honest, less stubborn, and more loving. Having more faith and trust in herself would also help.

Question 11: Final outcome?

Answer: 8 of Wands. Meredith has the strength to do all of the things suggested by this reading. She can work and have the active social life she seeks. The more positively she thinks and believes, the quicker her soul mate will arrive.

Comment: Creative visualization and meditation are two keys to success. A few minutes a day, every day, will bring your heart's desire to you. Meredith must be serious about wanting her soul mate in her life. If she is, she will prove it by using some of her time in meditation or creative visualization every day. Positive thinking and your beliefs manifest your life. Do it and reap your rewards now!

Soul Mate Spread for Josey

CARDS IN THE SPREAD

1st	position	2 of Pentacles
2nd	position	Ace of Cups (Reversed)
3rd	position	3 of Cups
4th	position	3 of Pentacles (Reversed)
5th	position	Queen of Swords
6th	position	Knight of Wands
7th	position	The Hermit
8th	position	2 of Cups (Reversed)
9th	position	Ace of Swords
10th	position	King of Swords
11th	position	3 of Wands

READING

Question 1: How do I contact my soul mate?

Answer: 2 of Pentacles. Josey must learn to balance her physical and material needs with her spiritual values. She must keep herself healthy and have faith in herself. The contact between Josey and her soul mate will occur when she is ready and balanced.

Question 2: Is my soul mate in the physical world now?

Answer: Ace of Cups (Reversed). According to this card, Josey is not receptive to the appearance of her soul mate. She is emotionally unstable, feels drained, and is quarreling with family members. This is not a time for new beginnings in love or new relationships.

Question 3: Is it possible to communicate with my soul mate now?

Answer: 3 of Cups. Communication with Josey's soul mate is possible and it will make her happy to make this contact. This can be an upbeat time for her, and getting involved with her creative side would be beneficial rather than the negative experiences that are happening to her through family members.

Question 4: What can I do to bring my soul mate into my life?

Answer: 3 of Pentacles (Reversed). Josey lacks faith in her abilities. Money will not bring her soul mate into her life experience. Josey must be happy, enjoying life, and feeling that life is worthwhile. She must believe that it is possible to encounter her soul mate.

Question 5: Is my soul mate a free spirit?

Answer: Queen of Swords. This Queen is independent, alone, and seeking a relationship. In this position, this card could indicate that Josey's soul mate is a passive, loving, and caring individual, while Josey is more aggressive and independent. Perhaps Josey can learn to control her aggression and spend more time exploring her feminine side.

Question 6: Have we been in relationships in the past?

Answer: Knight of Wands. This card indicates that Josey and her soul mate have communicated with each other, either in the past or in the present. This would show that they have had a relationship.

Question 7: Do I need to study or learn anything about soul mates?

Answer: The Hermit. Josey must learn to trust and respect herself and then she will be closer to encountering her soul mate. She would be wise to seek her inner teacher for spiritual guidance. Meditation can also help her contact her soul mate.

Question 8: Will there be harmony and well-being between us?

Answer: 2 of Cups (Reversed). Josey knows that she fears commitment and being hurt in love. She is not trusting and this has created emotional problems in her relationships. If there is no trust in a relationship, there is no need for that relationship, except to learn from it. How can there be harmony or well-being if there is no love or trust?

Question 9: How can I learn to love and accept my soul mate?

Answer: Ace of Swords. Josey must learn to love and accept herself first. Understanding herself is her first lesson and will change her beliefs. If she focuses her attention on her soul mate she is neglecting herself. Josey lacks trust—a main ingredient in a relationship. This card can show a loss, not a good beginning for a romantic relationship.

Question 10: What changes can I make while I wait for my soul mate?

Answer: King of Swords. Josey must use discrimination in deciding about changes. She must not get too emotionally involved with her family or other relationships. By maintaining her balance and learning to love, and respecting herself, she can attract her soul mate. She can make these changes by altering her beliefs and watching her thought patterns.

Question 11: Final outcome?

Answer: 3 of Wands. Creative visualization is a method that Josey could use to change her thinking. She is very creative and makes her professional and social lives. Now Josey needs to seek inner guidance for future plans that include her soul mate. New ideas will bring success and happiness to Josey if she believes in herself.

Comment: Josey is a Leo, sign of the ego. She becomes disappointed when her expectations do not turn out the way she wants them to. She is very creative and works at a job she loves. Josey has family problems and relationship blues—but problems are opportunities for growth and we must accept our experiences in a positive manner.

Chapter 9

JUST FOR FUN

IN THIS CHAPTER THERE ARE FOUR SPREADS; three have case studies and the fourth does not. Everyone will love the "Wish" spread—who does not have millions of wishes? The "Magical Lottery" spread will be popular and could work out very well for someone who has enough faith.

The spreads are:

>   Wish Spread
>
>   Yes or No
>
>   Magical Lottery Spread
>
>   Through the Week

The "Yes or No" spread is self-explanatory. and only eight cards are needed. In the spread "Through the Week," there are seven cards, one for each day. If you read the spread on Thursday, begin the reading with that day and go through the next week until you have covered seven days.

Try them all and see what results you come up with. Enjoy!

WISH SPREAD

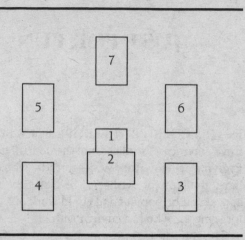

1. What is my wish?
2. Do I feel I deserve my wish?
3. Forces opposing my wish?
4. Forces working for me to help attain my wish?
5. Are there changes I must make to get my wish?
6. Is this wish in my best interest?
7. Outcome?

Wish Spread for Lorna

CARDS IN THE SPREAD

1st	position	Ace of Pentacles (Reversed)
2nd	position	Fool
3rd	position	Hanged Man
4th	position	2 of Pentacles (Reversed)
5th	position	Emperor (Reversed)
6th	position	7 of Swords
7th	position	Hierophant (Reversed)

READING

Question 1: What is my wish?

Answer: Ace of Pentacles (Reversed). Lorna is involved in her neighborhood watch program and is very unhappy with the circumstances involved. She feels there will be no new beginnings regarding the problem and that it will not go away. Lorna also feels that the property values in her neighborhood are affected by the undesirables who roam the streets where she lives. The thought of moving has occurred to Lorna, but this card says "no new beginnings with money," which would make moving into a new area at this time unlikely.

Question 2: Do I feel I deserve my wish?

Answer: Fool. Lorna's wish is to have others participate as much as she does, but this is a vain hope. She deserves to have support from her neighbors because they are also at risk. Lorna has a full-time job and a fourteen-year-old son at home, which keeps her quite busy.

Question 3: Forces opposing my wish?

Answer: Hanged Man. Lorna feels she must dedicate a lot of time policing the immediate area and attending meetings, but does not think that others are doing their share. She is sacrificing her will to the desires of others and this is making her ill. Lorna must keep her balance through meditation and creative visualization.

Question 4: Forces working for me to help attain my wish?

Answer: 2 of Pentacles (Reversed). Lorna is depressed because she would like to move. Her financial affairs will not allow her to do so at this time. What Lorna must understand is that she must work out this problem where she is and not take it with her if she does move. This card indicates a person who does not know how to budget money. Either Lorna is a spendthrift or her husband handles their financial affairs. Money and health balance each other, and we all benefit from this balance.

Question 5: Are there changes I must make to get my wish?

Answer: Emperor (Reversed). Lorna does not realize that she is good material for being the leader, authority figure, and spokesperson for her neighborhood. It is natural for most people to let the other person do it. Lorna should not let resentment, fear, or immature thinking cloud her vision. Perhaps a meeting and an election would stimulate her neighbors to take a larger share in the watch program.

Question 6: Is this wish in my best interest?

Answer: 7 of Swords. This card shows the path to mental thinking and control. It refers to problems and troubles that Lorna creates for herself, which are temporary. Their house has been burglarized twice and Lorna feels uncomfortable whenever she is away. Her belief system is attracting her experiences but she is reluctant to accept the responsibility for events. She is capable of being the spokeswoman for the neighborhood watch program, but the choice is hers. Lorna would know what is going on if she stayed with the group and that would be in her best interest.

Question 7: Outcome?

Answer: Hierophant (Reversed). Lorna does not believe in an inner source. She is a Cancer and desires safety, security, and survival. This is a materialistic view and rarely satisfies the soul. Meditation and creative visualization could be the answer to her prayers if she would only try.

Comment: Lorna is a school psychologist and along with her job she has a husband, a son, and her big house to take care of. She may be pushing to move although she loves her home. Most of her friends live in a different area—perhaps this factor is the most important clue of all! There are four Major Arcana cards in this spread, which may indicate that four individuals play an important role in Lorna's life at this time. With faith, Lorna may get her wish *and* move!

Wish Spread for Fred

CARDS IN THE SPREAD

1st	position	4 of Cups
2nd	position	2 of Wands
3rd	position	Moon
4th	position	Ace of Cups (Reversed)
5th	position	3 of Cups (Reversed)
6th	position	7 of Cups
7th	position	7 of Wands

READING

Question 1: What is my wish?

Answer: 4 of Cups. Fred realizes his ability to love and that he must balance his emotions. Fred is a Scorpio, a water sign, and very intense. There is constant turmoil in his life between his business and his family. Looking at the cards in this spread we see the focus is on love and emotional needs on one hand, and business on the other. Fred's wish is for balance in all areas. There is a tendency to hang on to past experiences that he must release now to get his wish.

Question 2: Do I feel I deserve my wish?

Answer: 2 of Wands. Fred knows his work and how to get along socially. He has the world in his hands. He is a successful businessman and his wife and sister are both involved in the business. Fred feels he deserves his good fortune and strives for balance all the time.

Question 3: Forces opposing my wish?

Answer: Moon. On some level, Fred will not face the truth. His wife and sister are in competition for his affections and this is creating problems. He needs to use his psychic abilities (water sign) to maintain peace and harmony between these two. Fred might be swayed first one way and then the other by his own emotional needs. The Moon card also refers to Fred's mother. Fred and his sister lost their mother when they were very young. This has created an emotional bond between brother and sister, which would be difficult to break. Attainment is also a reachable goal for Fred.

Question 4: Forces working for me to help attain my wish?

Answer: Ace of Cups (Reversed). Fred may feel a little unstable but he will not have any new beginnings in emotional affairs. He may not be aware of his emotions being drained either. Fred's business is becoming more and more successful, so there are material forces helping him to victory.

Question 5: Are there changes I must make to get my wish?

Answer: 3 of Cups (Reversed). This card tells us that Fred does not make himself happy in love. He is having difficulty in his relationships and it is causing an emotional drain, some depression, and the potential for loss. Perhaps Fred feels lonely due to the problems with his family. The initial change Fred could make is to be happy and count his blessings.

The women in his life will have to work out their problems of jealousy and resentment without his help.

Question 6: Is this wish in my best interest?

Answer: 7 of Cups. This card refers to victory in love. If Fred keeps his mental control, the balance he is seeking will happen. Fred has a good imagination and through his creative thinking he has found success. Fred's success has brought him material well-being from which his wife and sister naturally benefit. So, while his business has helped everyone materially, it doesn't always help emotionally.

Question 7: Outcome?

Answer: 7 of Wands. Fred must take the mental path, which speaks of control, in his work and social activities. Victory and balance are then assured in both directions. He must rely on his own judgment, but not act egotistically or feel superior. Success will continue and balance will save the day!

Comment: Fred has worked very hard for his success and his wife and sister have been instrumental in helping him achieve it. Perhaps it is good that Fred travels a good deal for this business. As long as each person is getting some of their ego needs met, everything will be fine. Pulling together would make success even sweeter.

Wish Spread for Ken

CARDS IN THE SPREAD

1st	position	3 of Pentacles
2nd	position	10 of Cups
3rd	position	Queen of Swords (Reversed)
4th	position	Page of Cups (Reversed)
5th	position	Page of Pentacles (Reversed)
6th	position	5 of Wands (Reversed)
7th	position	Page of Wands

READING

Question 1: What is my wish?

Answer: 3 of Pentacles. Ken is a lawyer. He makes money because he is good at what he does. He feels he is a master craftsman and very creative. Ken's wish is to remain productive and take care of his family's needs and his own.

Question 2: Do I feel I deserve my wish?

Answer: 10 of Cups. Ken is having some change in his love and emotional state. This is Ken's second marriage and new family. If there is joy in the home then Ken feels he deserves his wish. His children from his first marriage are all adults and able to take care of their own needs.

Question 3: Forces opposing my wish?

Answer: Queen of Swords (Reversed). This Queen has problems and troubles but may not wish to confront them. She has been married but is now divorced. This is Ken's sister who does not care for

Ken's new wife and tries to create trouble between them. Ken tries to maintain a balance with these two women and is not always successful. There is a certain amount of jealousy involved as Ken's new wife is much younger than Ken. Fortunately, Ken knows his sister well and understands that she is a manipulator.

Question 4: Forces working for me to help attain my wish?

Answer: Page of Cups (Reversed). This Page shows an emotional drain and many disappointments—but also great expectations. Ken has three children from his first marriage and his son was constantly in trouble. Now Ken has a second son who is very young and lovable. This boy may be the force that is working for Ken to help him attain his wish.

Question 5: Are there changes I must make to get my wish?

Answer: Page of Pentacles (Reversed). This Page is not interested in getting an education, setting goals, or learning how to earn money to be independent. This could refer to the older son who wants the easy life, dislikes authority, and has been involved with drugs. Changes that Ken must make concern this son. Perhaps he feels rejected by Ken since he was young when his parents divorced. Showing love to this son may create the changes Ken needs to get his wish and also help the young man.

Question 6: Is this wish in my best interest?

Answer: 5 of Wands (Reversed). Ken feels that he

has been very fortunate in his life. He does not appear as confident now and is afraid that his relationship will not remain as happy as it has been. Ken's ideas about work and the social scene have changed and his beliefs are also different. His wish for financial success is positive and by affirming prosperity his circumstances should not change. Ken's health has been good and by keeping a positive outlook, it should remain so.

Question 7: Outcome?

Answer: Page of Wands. This Page is eager to experience work and social activities. The Page is headstrong, desires freedom, and is independent. Ken said this described one of his daughters whom he is very proud of. His other daughter has turned out fine, as well. Ken realizes he has another chance with his young son and hopes to do a better job this time.

Comment: It is difficult to start raising a child when the parent is in his fifties. Many people are having second families as a way to stay young minded. Ken loves all of his children, but was not always there to cater to their needs. When parents and children have high expectations for each other it is a set-up for disappointment. All a person can do is try to do the best that they can, which Ken feels he is doing.

YES OR NO

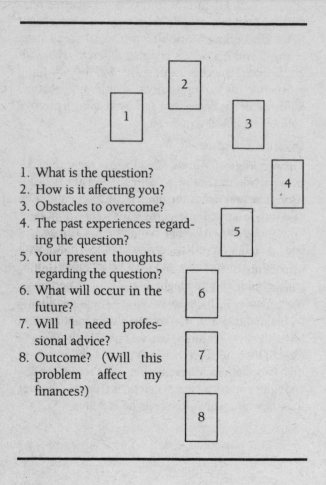

1. What is the question?
2. How is it affecting you?
3. Obstacles to overcome?
4. The past experiences regarding the question?
5. Your present thoughts regarding the question?
6. What will occur in the future?
7. Will I need professional advice?
8. Outcome? (Will this problem affect my finances?)

Yes or No for Polly

CARDS IN THE SPREAD

1st	position	9 of Cups
2nd	position	5 of Wands
3rd	position	Hierophant (Reversed)
4th	position	Wheel of Fortune (Reversed)
5th	position	4 of Swords
6th	position	7 of Pentacles
7th	position	Queen of Wands
8th	position	High Priestess

READING

Question 1: What is the question?

Answer: 9 of Cups. This is the wish card and it is upright, which indicates Polly will get her wish. It also shows that Polly has gained wisdom through her experiences. She relies on her inner teacher (Hermit) and is guided by the Light. Her question pertains to going into partnership with her friend. Polly has tried several times to work with female partners but has never been successful. She realizes this problem stems from her relationship with her mother. Polly needs to find a man to partner with and even that may not work out.

Question 2: How is it affecting you?

Answer: 5 of Wands. Polly and her friend each want their own way in this venture. They each believe they have the best way to do things at work and socially.

This ego focus could cause problems. She is constantly finding fault with her friend, which is not a good sign.

Question 3: Obstacles to overcome?

Answer: Hierophant (Reversed). Polly does not wish to follow any rules or regulations in her venture. She is a rebel and desires to do things her way and could be putting stumbling blocks in her own path with this attitude. Polly wants to control all aspects of her venture and having a partner may not be the answer.

Question 4: The past experiences regarding the question?

Answer: Wheel of Fortune (Reversed). Polly should not gamble or take chances with her venture. In the past she had partners and felt they all took advantage of her. She still believes that she will attract someone who will do the same thing to her now. With this belief, she should not get involved with a partner of any kind.

Question 5: The present thoughts regarding the question?

Answer: 4 of Swords. Polly must realize that she should rest and meditate on her problems. She needs to put herself in balance and realize she is creating her own experiences. Her ego is driving her and she must recognize this fact. There is also a jealous factor in the three swords hanging over the figure and she is creating these problems herself.

Question 6: What will occur in the future?

Answer: 7 of Pentacles. The mental path to money. This shows Polly that she can have money and will have to make decisions about what to do with it. Polly's ego was a problem in the past. The money may come suddenly and she needs to be prepared.

Question 7: Will I need professional advice?

Answer: Queen of Wands. Polly wants to do it all herself. She must seek legal counsel for her new venture if she wants to protect herself and her product. This card indicates the ego in work and social life. Polly wants to be a star, to be admired and praised. If this card represents the partner, Polly must proceed with caution!

Question 8: Outcome? (Will this problem affect my finances?)

Answer: High Priestess. The High Priestess says "I know." This card indicates that Polly has the answer to her question within her. She is intelligent and if she does not let her need for money or her ego get in the way, success is assured.

Comment: Polly would like to change her occupation. Her new venture looks promising and could make her a winner. She must follow legal procedure, even if she is a rebel. The future looks bright for her.

Yes or No for Darla

CARDS IN THE SPREAD

1st	position	4 of Pentacles (Reversed)
2nd	position	8 of Pentacles (Reversed)
3rd	position	Chariot (Reversed)
4th	position	5 of Pentacles
5th	position	7 of Cups (Reversed)
6th	position	10 of Pentacles (Reversed)
7th	position	6 of Swords (Reversed)
8th	position	Justice

READING

Question 1: What is the question?

Answer: 4 of Pentacles (Reversed). There is a lack of balance in Darla's mental attitude. Her sense of money is also out of balance, although she is not greedy. Her thinking is materially based and not especially spiritual. Her question concerned her job and if she would still be working in the same place in September.

Question 2: How is it affecting you?

Answer: 8 of Pentacles (Reversed). Darla feels she is working with cheaters and dishonest people and she senses a lack of strength within herself to deal with them. Darla is trying to put her finances in better shape, so she needs the job. Health problems can arise if she feels powerless, but Darla is a strong Scorpio and very capable of holding her own in most situations.

Question 3: Obstacles to overcome?

Answer: Chariot (Reversed). This card refers to the material path. Darla may feel she is not in control of her desires or finances. She may not be aware of her inner source who is there to guide her if she has the faith. Darla may not feel secure or nurtured at this time.

Question 4: The past experiences regarding the question?

Answer: 5 of Pentacles. Darla believed in money and made it her god. This is a crippling belief and does not show a prosperity mind. However, she has put this belief in her past and has learned through experience that it is not healthy. Darla is good at what she does and need not fear losing her job.

Question 5: Your present thought regarding the question?

Answer: 7 of Cups (Reversed). Darla is emotionally drained due to a conflict that took place at work. Perhaps if Darla were to creatively visualize herself starting the new semester in September, she would feel more secure and assured about her teaching job.

Question 6: What will occur in the future?

Answer: 10 of Pentacles (Reversed). There are no changes in the money department for Darla. She is working and understands that she must cut back on her desires and pay off her bills. This could take some pressure off and stop the worries in the future.

Question 7: Will I need professional advice?

Answer: 6 of Swords (Reversed). Darla may need to employ a lawyer, but not at this time. Darla is not making choices right now and she must stay and face her problems. She must also use her mind to analyze her problems and troubles and not allow others to make decisions for her.

Question 8: Outcome? (Will this problem affect my finances?)

Answer: Justice. Yes, it could affect her finances. Darla may need legal advice (scales of Justice), or she just wants to be treated fairly. If there is a legal suit, it is likely she would win.

Comment: Darla has four pentacle cards in her spread, which shows money is a prime factor in her life. She also has many reversed cards. These are not all negative, but to have so many in a spread has much meaning. Darla must change some of her beliefs in order to change her life. Meditation helps to root out negative habit patterns and Darla would benefit greatly from this.

MAGICAL LOTTERY SPREAD

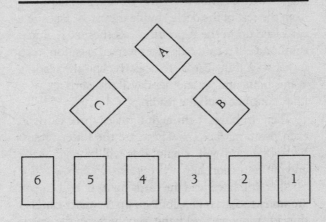

A: Is this a good day to buy a ticket on the lottery?

B. Obstacles to overcome?

C. Querent's mental attitude toward wining the lottery.

1 through 6: These cards will provide the numbers to play in the lottery.

TO USE THIS SPREAD

For this spread, you will use only the twenty-two Major Arcana cards. After you have separated them from the rest of the deck, shuffle the cards. Place one card face up in the A position, another on B, and a third on C. If a card falls in a reversed position, read it that way. If the cards are negative, end the reading at this point and try another day. If the cards are positive, continue with the reading.

Then, in boxes 1 through 6, place three cards in each position, face up. These are the lottery numbers. One card will remain; this will be read at the end of the session.

After you have read the cards on A, B, and C, you are ready to start on box 1. Pick up the three cards in this position and add the numbers of the cards together. Do not reduce the number values of any cards. If the total is over the limit of the lottery, stop the reading and try another day.

Example: Box 1 may contain The Moon, Hierophant, and Justice.

The Moon	18
Hierophant	5
Justice	11
	34

The amount of this box would be 34, which is within the number range of the lottery.

Pick up the three cards on Box 2 and add them in the same way. Repeat this with the rest of the boxes, adding each box separately. When you are finished, there will be a total for each of the six boxes. Next, turn over the last card to get the final message.

The application of the final card is up to you. If it is a low numbered card—The Magician (1) or High Priestess (2)— you may wish to substitute it for one of the six numbers gained through adding the Major Arcana cards in the six piles of the reading. Because you have added the values of the numbers in these piles, it is impossible to play a 1 or 2 in the lottery simply using those numbers.

If the totals in each of the six boxes are within lottery limits, go buy a ticket. Do not wait for another day—do it now!

Remember, when the cards are in the boxes numbered 1 through 6, they can be upright or reversed. When the cards are in boxes A, B, C, they must be read the way they are found—upright or reversed—on the box.

Magical Lottery for Arlene

CARDS IN THE SPREAD

1st position	The Devil (Reversed)	
2nd position	Sun (Reversed)	
3rd position	The Fool (Reversed)	
Box 1	Wheel of Fortune	10
	Death	13
	High Priestess	2
Box 2	The Tower	16
	Judgment	20
	Chariot	7
Box 3	Magician	1
	Hierophant	5
	The World	21
Box 4	Hanged Man	12
	Empress	3
	Emperor	4
Box 5	Lovers	6
	Temperance	14
	The Moon	18
Box 6	Hermit	9
	Star	17
	Justice	11
Last card	Strength	8

READING:

Question 1: Is this a good day to buy a ticket on the lottery?

Answer: The Devil (Reversed). Arlene is not as greedy for material possessions or as selfish as some others, but there is a block in her thinking that refuses to allow her the better things in life.

Question 2: Obstacles to overcome?

Answer: Sun (Reversed). Arlene has a lack of courage or confidence. She must learn to be open and honest with others, which builds trust and respect. Arlene places too much emphasis on the physical-sexual side of her life. This is the time to overcome past habit patterns of thought and learn to love oneself.

Question 3: Querent's mental attitude toward winning the lottery.

Answer: The Fool (Reversed). With this mental attitude Arlene is sabotaging her desires. She must balance her actions, pleasures, sexual needs, and selfishness by having faith in herself. If Arlene does not feel she deserves to win the lottery, how will she do it?

Box 1 Total — 25

Box 2 Total — 43

Box 3 Total — 27

Box 4 Total — 19

Box 5 Total — 38

Box 6 Total — 37

Because the final card of Arlene's reading was Strength, with a numerological value of 8, the number was disregarded and she played he six numbers from the boxes. However, it does indicate that she has the strength to overcome all obstacles and changer her life for the better.

Arlene bought a ticket on Saturday. Her reading was done on Thursday. She did not win anything.

Comment: Buy a ticket on the day you put out a positive spread. Good Luck!

THROUGH THE WEEK

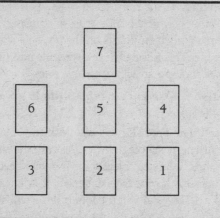

1. What new plans can I make for this day?
2. Will my plans include another person?
3. Will I enjoy this day? (Travel or be creative?)
4. Will I do good work today and be productive?
5. What changes or new experiences will I encounter today?
6. What new responsibilities or family issues will I be involved with today?
7. Will this be a day of rest or mental activity?

Worksheet for Tarot Spreads

TITLE OF SPREAD _____

1st card _____ key words _____

2nd card _____ key words _____

3rd card _____ key words _____

4th card _____ key words _____

5th card _____ key words _____

6th card _____ key words _____

7th card _____ key words _____

8th card _____ key words _____

9th card _____ key words _____

10th card _____ key words _____

11th card _____ key words _____

12th card _____ key words _____

13th card _____ key words _____

14th card _____ key words _____

15th card _____ key words _____

OUTSIDE INFLUENCES

Major Arcana   _____

Court Cards   _____

Combined Total _____
(people involved)

ELEMENTS

Wands   _____   Fire   _____

Cups   _____   Water _____

Pentacles _____   Earth _____

Swords   _____   Air   _____

REPEATED CARDS

1 _____   3 _____   5 _____   7 _____   9 _____

2 _____   4 _____   6 _____   8 _____   10 _____

REPEATED SIGNS

Aries   _____   Leo   _____   Sagittarius _____

Taurus   _____   Virgo   _____   Capricorn   _____

Gemini   _____   Libra   _____   Aquarius   _____

Cancer   _____   Scorpio _____   Pisces   _____

Worksheet for Tarot Spreads

TITLE OF SPREAD _____

1st card _____ key words _____

2nd card _____ key words _____

3rd card _____ key words _____

4th card _____ key words _____

5th card _____ key words _____

6th card _____ key words _____

7th card _____ key words _____

8th card _____ key words _____

9th card _____ key words _____

10th card _____ key words _____

11th card _____ key words _____

12th card _____ key words _____

13th card _____ key words _____

14th card _____ key words _____

15th card _____ key words _____

OUTSIDE INFLUENCES

Major Arcana   _____

Court Cards   _____

Combined Total _____
(people involved)

ELEMENTS

Wands   _____   Fire   _____

Cups   _____   Water   _____

Pentacles _____   Earth   _____

Swords   _____   Air   _____

REPEATED CARDS

1 _____   3 _____   5 _____   7 _____   9 _____

2 _____   4 _____   6 _____   8 _____   10 _____

REPEATED SIGNS

Aries   _____   Leo   _____   Sagittarius _____

Taurus _____   Virgo   _____   Capricorn   _____

Gemini _____   Libra   _____   Aquarius   _____

Cancer _____   Scorpio _____   Pisces   _____

Free Magazine

Read articles by Llewellyn authors, recommendations by experts, and information on new releases. To receive a **free** copy of Llewellyn's magazine, *New Worlds of Mind & Spirit*, simply call 1-877-NEW-WRLD or visit our website at www.llewellyn.com.

☽ LLEWELLYN ORDERING INFORMATION

Order Online:
Visit our website at www.llewellyn.com, select your books, and order them on our secure server.

Order by Phone:
- Call toll-free within the U.S. at 1-877-NEW-WRLD (1-877-639-9753). Call toll-free within Canada at 1-866-NEW-WRLD (1-866-639-9753)
- We accept VISA, MasterCard, and American Express

Order by Mail:
Send the full price of your order (MN residents add 7% sales tax) in U.S. funds, plus postage & handling to:

Llewellyn Worldwide
P.O. Box 64383, Dept. 1-56718-002-7
St. Paul, MN 55164-0383, U.S.A.

Postage & Handling:
Standard (U.S., Mexico, & Canada). If your order is:
$49.99 & under, add $3.00
$50.00 & over, free standard shipping

AK, HI & PR: $15.00 for one book plus $1.00 for each additional book

International Orders: (airmail only)
$16.00 for one book plus $3.00 for each additional book

*Orders are processed within 2 business days.
Please allow for normal shipping time. Postage and handling rates
subject to change.*

Robin Wood Tarot Deck

*Created and illustrated
by Robin Wood*

*Instructions by Robin Wood
and Michael Short*

Tap into the wisdom of your subconscious with one of the most beautiful Tarot decks on the market today! Reminiscent of the Rider-Waite deck, the *Robin Wood Tarot* is flavored with enchanting nature imagery and luminous energies. Even the novice reader will find these cards easy and enjoyable to interpret.

Radiant and rich, these cards were illustrated with a unique technique that brings out the resplendent color of the prismacolor pencils. The cards are printed in quality card stock and boxed complete with instruction booklet, which provides the upright and reversed meanings of each card, as well as three basic card layouts. Beautiful and brilliant, the *Robin Wood Tarot* is a must-have deck.

**0-87542-894-0
boxed: 78 cards w/booklet** $19.95